Personal

By the same author:
THE ESP WORKBOOK
FORTUNE-TELLING BY ASTROLOGY
FORTUNE-TELLING BY PALMISTRY
FORTUNE-TELLING WITH NUMBERS
HOW TO READ FACES

PERSONAL SECRETS

Seventy Ways to Know Yourself and Others

Rodney Davies

The Aquarian Press
An Imprint of HarperCollins*Publishers*

The Aquarian Press
An Imprint of Grafton Books
A Division of HarperCollins*Publishers*
77-85 Fulham Palace Road,
Hammersmith, London W6 8JB

Published by The Aquarian Press 1991

1   3   5   7   9   10   8   6   4   2

All illustrations in the book are by the author

British Library Cataloguing in Publication Data
Davies, Rodney
Personal secrets: seventy ways to know yourself
and others.
1. Physiognomy
I. Title
138

ISBN 1-85538-044-7

Typesetting by MJL Limited, Hitchin, Hertfordshire

Printed and bound in Great Britain by
Collins, Glasgow

The Kingdom of Heaven is within you and whosoever knoweth himself shall find it.

From *The Oxyrhyncus Sayings of Jesus*

CONTENTS

INTRODUCTION

Know then thyself, presume not God to scan;
The proper study of Mankind is Man.*

It is to the ancient Greeks that we owe the wisdom of self-knowledge, and indeed it was to their most civilized god Apollo that this most civilized of races linked the maxim 'Know thyself', by which association they hoped to persuade all their fellows to do just that. For the Greeks realized that without knowledge of oneself, without understanding who one is, each person is essentially a lost soul, driven hither and thither by irrational urges and longings, forever stumbling from the path of rightness and goodness. That path is the Middle Way, which lies between the opposites of existence, whose excessive qualities constantly tempt us, and to which, if we do not know our weaknesses, we are likely to fall prey.

Yet self-knowledge is not something that is easily acquired. In fact the Greeks believed that not even Apollo was born with this divine attribute, but had to learn it through his own mistakes. They said that it was only after he had been punished for his excesses by being made to serve King Admetus for one year as a simple shepherd, that Lord Apollo

* The quotations at the beginning of each chapter are all taken from the works of Alexander Pope (1688-1744).

gained wisdom and thereafter urged his followers to 'Know thyself' and 'Avoid excess', and that 'The Mean is Best'.

Hence this book has been written to help you, the reader, to gain insights into both yourself and other people. The methods described are both traditional and modern, and have the advantage of being neither stuffy nor abstruse. They will appeal to everyone, although the young should find them particularly useful and instructive.

Chapter One
BODY TYPES

Presumptious Man! the reason wouldst thou find,
Why form'd so weak, so little and so blind?

The art of knowing a person from his or her appearance or
body type is known as physiognomy, a word deriving from
two Greek roots, *phusis* or 'nature' and *gnomen* or 'judge',
and hence means 'judging of a man's nature'. It was defined
by Francis Bacon as the 'discoverer of the disposition of the
mind from the lineaments of the body'. In a narrow sense
such judgement is made from the features of the face, but
originally the term included the whole outer form of a person, as well as his or her stance, way of walking, voice type,
etc. We shall be dealing with physiognomy in its widest sense
throughout this book.

Physiognomy is an ancient practice, dating back well before
the birth of Jesus Christ, yet this does not mean that its central thesis—*as without, so within*—is necessarily suspect or
false. Indeed, certain modern psychologists, as we shall see,
believe that man's outer form reflects his inner nature, and
the estimation of temperament from behaviour is a well-
known axiom of science.

The first treatise on physiognomy of which we know was
written by Aristotle (384-22 BC), and is titled *Displaying the
Secrets of Nature Relating to Physiognomy*. In this work, apart
from discussing the meanings of the facial features and other
aspects of the appearance, the great philosopher briefly

Figure 1: Aristotle, the great philosopher

describes seven body types and outlines the character traits possessed by each. But his observations pertain only to the male physique, for of the woman he asks, 'Does physiognomy give the same judgement on her, as it does to the man who is like unto her?—to which he replies, 'By no means, but far otherwise; in regard that the conception of the woman is much different from that of the man, even in those respects which are said to be common.' Thus Aristotle, despite his genius, was a male chauvinist, as were most of his contemporaries.

But we shall none the less begin our study of human character by recording Aristotle's seven types of person and his comments about their temperaments.

1

If you are tall, slim of build, and stand up straight, Aristotle says this means that you have a somewhat reprehensible character, being proud, cruel, assertive, confident, stingy, deceitful, hard to please, often malicious, and find it difficult to forgive a wrong.

Should you be very tall and slim, or in other words like a bean-pole, your physique identifies you as 'a projecting man' or the type of person who pushes himself and his ideas upon others. You like both to laugh at your own jokes and to have your own way. Yet your selfishness, Aristotle warns, is not likely to bring you any good.

However, if you are short in stature, yet slim and upright, then your character is very much better, as you are 'wise and ingenious, bold and confident, of good understanding,' although you have 'a deceitful heart'.

But should you be short and fat, or thickset, it means that you are not very bright, and are vain, superstitious, envious, suspicious of others, and find it hard to forget a wrong done to you.

If you are tall and fat, Aristotle claims that this identifies you as being generous and brave, yet also rather unintelligent, ungrateful, and inclined to get others into trouble.

If your posture is bad, so that you stoop, it means that you are a person lacking in fluency and style. You are also secretive and incredulous, and thus too easily believe all that you hear.

And lastly, if you have a large stomach, it marks you out as being jovial and sociable, but lacking in will power.

In the century before Aristotle's birth another Greek philosopher, Empedocles, had argued that the world and everything in it is composed of four 'root-substances' or elements,
namely Air, Fire, Earth, and Water, which therefore con-
stituted ultimate reality. This led Hippocrates of Cos (c.460-
377 BC), the 'father of medicine', to postulate that the elements manifested themselves within the human body as the
four life-giving fluids or *humours*, these being blood, yellow
bile, black bile, and phlegm.

When the humours are present in balanced quantities, said
Hippocrates, the result is good health, a beautiful body, and
an equable temperament. But the ideal balance is seldom
achieved. It is more common to find one of the humours
predominating, whose characteristics become impressed
upon the physical body, thereby giving rise to a particular
body type and temperament. Hence those with an excess
of blood (or Air) have a sanguine physique and temperament; of yellow bile (or Fire), a choleric physique and temperament; of black bile (or Earth), a melancholic physique
and temperament; and of phlegm (or Water), a phlegmatic
physique and temperament.

But although pure Hippocratic types are also quite rare,
as we are normally more mixed, it is useful to give a sum-
mary of the principal physical and temperamental features
of the four types.

2

The *sanguine* person is of medium height, with a strong, well-
built and attractive body, and a healthily pink, although
sometimes flushed, complexion. If you have such an outer
form, then you are probably naturally cheerful and optimistic, easy-going and sociable, and have an intelligent mind.
But because you also have a strong sex-drive, you tend to
be preoccupied with affairs of the heart and thus liable to
contract venereal infections.

The *choleric* person is typically quite tall, with a lean and
hairy body, and a yellowish complexion. If you have such

an appearance, it reveals that you are bold, shrewd, energetic, and ambitious. Hence you are a get-up-and-go-type, who hates to be held back or frustrated. You have a bad temper and an aggressive manner. It is therefore not surprising that you are likely to suffer from heart ailments.

The *melancholic* person is of medium height, or shorter, and has a strong, well-developed body. The complexion is olive, the hair thick and dark or black in colour, and the movements are slow and purposeful. Should this description fit you, you have a dour and pessimistic temperament, and although you work hard, you are a plodder. You are happiest and most at ease in your home surroundings. You are prone to depression, and to pleurisy and other lung disorders.

Lastly, the *phlegmatic* person is of medium height, or taller, with a shapeless body lacking any muscular definition. The colouring is fair, the hair is fine and lank, and the expression somewhat vacuous. Should you possess such an appearance, it identifies you as a placid and apathetic person, who lacks much interest in life or ambition, and who is content to lead a quiet, uneventful existence. You are susceptible to epilepsy, dysentery, and feverish ailments.

Each of Aristotle's seven physical types, briefly sketched though they were by him, later became identified with one or other of the seven planets of traditional astrology, viz. the Moon, Mercury, Venus, the Sun, Mars, Jupiter, and Saturn. This led to their various characteristics being more clearly defined. You may be able to recognize your planetary type from among the descriptions given below.

3

(1) The Moon or Luna person is typically above average height, often fat or flabby, and has rather large feet. The head is round, as is the face. The complexion is colourless, the eyes blue, watery, and staring, and the hair blond or brown

in colour and lacking in body. The small nose is upturned. The mouth and ears are also small, the latter being set close to the head.

If you have these physical features, you are likely also to be imaginative, idealistic and selfish, but because you are lazy and quickly bored, you find it hard either to complete tasks or to work towards long-term goals. However, you enjoy travel, especially to exotic and faraway places, and you have sufficient artistic talent to enable you to make a living as a poet, writer, musician or composer. You love nature and the sea, and you prefer to live alone.

You are attracted to any occupation involving liquids, particularly to work aboard ships, to nursing and the other caring professions, and to restaurant employment, teaching, interior design, dress designing and manufacture, bartending, catering, estate agencing, the Church, the law, and related fields.

(2) The Mercury person, by contrast, is short in stature—he or she seldom exceeds five feet eight inches in height—and has a lean, wiry frame. The face is triangular, the forehead high and broad, the features rectangular, and the chin pointed. The eyes are dark, bright, and restless, and the whites have a yellowish hue. The complexion may be olive. The expression is alert and changeable. The chest is large, and the manner of moving is quick, confident, and graceful.

If this seems to be describing your physical type, then you probably also possess a quick, intelligent mind and a ready tongue. Indeed, you love arguing and persuading. You also enjoy studying and learning, and you have a retentive memory. But because you are anxious and impatient, you are ill-equipped for waiting. You need quick results! You have many acquaintances and you are skilled at handling others, but you have few close friendships. In fact emotional closeness scares you, which is why some find you flighty and insincere. And you are not all that interested in sex.

You like making money and you are good at business, although you are better at planning and scheming than you are at sticking with the job. However, you are prepared to

Figure 2: Nancy Reagan, a Mercury type

take risks, which can sometimes pay off handsomely. You also function well in any occupation that allows you to express yourself and to utilize your considerable powers of persuasion, such as teaching, buying and selling, public relations, law, counselling, acting, journalism, conducting tourists, and so forth. You are also naturally good at handling dogs and horses.

(3) The Venus person is the most attractive of the seven types. He or she is of medium height, although sometimes shorter, with a gracefully formed, well-proportioned, sexy

Figure 3: Contralto Kathleen Ferrier, a Venus type

figure. The face is oval, the forehead high, and the hair fine, wavy and abundant. The complexion is a healthy pink. The large eyes are blue or light brown in colour and have long, curling lashes. The cheeks are round and dimpled. The full, red lips part frequently to smile, displaying white, even teeth. The bosom is full in the woman, the chest large in the man.

You are fortunate if you have such a figure, as you have little difficulty in attracting admirers and lovers. And your manner and personality are equally charming, for you are naturally cheerful and bright, kind and unassuming. You enjoy social occasions; indeed, you are at your best in company, as you tend to get depressed when alone. You are also honest and unselfish, yet because you are somewhat lazy and lacking in drive, you are essentially a dependent type. You are motivated chiefly by romance and lovemaking.

You are drawn to jobs which are glamorous and which involve you with other people, particularly to those connected with the arts, with fashion and beauty, and, perhaps not surprisingly, with health care. Thus you find hairdressing, selling perfume, flowers, cosmetics, etc., modelling, dress designing, acting and entertaining, doing make-up, and massaging appealing. You also have skills as a mediator and as a counsellor. However, you hate to get your hands dirty.

(4) The Sun person is also of medium height, yet has a more athletic and masculine physique than the Venus person. He or she has a triangular face, with regular, well-formed features. The complexion is clear, fresh, and pink. The forehead is narrow but quite high, and the hair is thick, wavy, and dark in colour. The blue or brown eyes are large and sparkling, like those of the Venus type. The straight nose has well-proportioned nostrils. The jaw is wide and strong. The medium-sized ears lie close to the head. The chest is broad and full, and the legs are long and well-muscled.

If you have such a physique and appearance, then you will also possess plenty of energy and drive, and a cheerful, outgoing, yet somewhat hot-tempered, disposition. You have your own opinions, and you are not at all shy about

Figure 4: Anne Charleston, who plays Madge Bishop in 'Neighbours', a Sun type

speaking your mind. Indeed, you are a natural leader and organizer, and you can handle responsibility.

You thrive in any field that puts you in the public eye, as you like to be noticed, and you are particularly drawn to acting, politics, and entertainment. You also, however, make a good businessman, lawyer, union leader, architect, physician, and teacher or lecturer. You are fascinated by gold and by royalty, perhaps to the extent of dealing in the former and working for the latter.

Figure 5: Boxer Mike Tyson, a Mars type

(5) The Mars person is of average height and is distinguished by his or her strong and robust physique. The posture is good: the spine is kept straight, the shoulders back, and the head erect. The face is square and the complexion ruddy. The neck is short and thick. The gaze is keen and alert, but the eyebrows press down too closely to the large eyes. The small ears are laid flat against the sides of the head. The legs are short but strong.

Should you have such a physique and appearance, you

will also be blessed with a lot of energy and verve, considerable self-confidence, a quick temper, and a stubborn manner. You like to get your own way, and you don't mind shouting to make your point. Yet while you want to win, you prefer to keep matters honest and above board. You are keen on games and sports, money, and lovemaking, although not necessarily in that order.

You are naturally attracted to work in the armed forces and the police, and to related jobs such as security guard, bodyguard, and night watchman. Animal slaughtering and butchering, weapons manufacturing, machinery repairing, animal training, farming and stockbroking are all fields that interest you. And while you could make a fine surgeon or veterinarian at the one extreme, so you could also make an equally good labourer, stone mason, carpenter or journeyman at the other.

(6) The Jupiter person is somewhat above average height and typically has a thick-set, fleshy, large-boned body. The rectangular face has a pleasant and kindly expression, and is distinguished by its arched eyebrows, large yet well-formed ears, and by the long, white teeth. The hair is fine and abundant, and brown in colour. He or she often flicks back his head in the manner of a horse, and has a loud, neighing laugh.

If this description matches your own, then you are also a warm-hearted, sociable person, who wants both to enjoy life and get ahead in your job or profession. You like being in charge and in fact you find it easy to control and direct others. But your love of the pleasures of life may encourage you to spend and party excessively, so harming both your financial and your physical health. Yet despite this, you are fundamentally a decent sort, who upholds the law and who is conscious of the wider dimension of the spirit.

You are naturally attracted to the professions, although you will not be entirely happy unless you rise right to the top. Politics and the Church are two other fields that interest you and for which you are well suited. You also make a capable editor and writer, travel agent, geologist, archaeologist, and

Figure 6: Model Jerry Hall, a Jupiter type

civil engineer. Indeed, you prefer work that gets you outdoors.

(7) The Saturn person is the tallest of the seven astrological or planetary types, and has a gaunt, bony physique. The face is long and vaguely volcano-shaped, the cheeks are thin, and the complexion has an unhealthy yellow hue. The sad eyes are partnered by bushy, dark eyebrows that often meet above the nose. The male frequently becomes bald. The ears are prominent, and the long, straight nose has large, yet stiff nostrils. The larynx is outstanding, the

shoulders are thin, and the arms are long.

Should you possess several of these features, then you are probably also an introverted, solitary person, who prefers your own company and thoughts. In fact you find it hard to smile, and you have little love in your heart for your fellow human beings. Your views are independent, sometimes eccentric, even perverse, which is why you seldom join any group or sect that has a rigid ideology. You are a hard, yet slow and methodical, worker. You are also prudent and cautious, and typically uneasy in the company of the opposite sex, although your sex drive is strong.

Because you love the outdoors and enjoy working with your hands, you are attracted to occupations like market gardening, park management, and farm labouring, and also to geology, oil exploration and extraction, and mining. Your interest in the dark, dead and dirty side of life admirably suits you for the following jobs: grave digger, mortuary attendant, crematorium worker, undertaker, rubbish collector, plumber, prison officer, laboratory assistant, sewerman, toilet attendant, etc.

These early and somewhat unsophisticated, although by no means wholly erroneous, attempts to classify people according to their physique and temperament, went largely unchallenged until the nineteenth century, when a more systematic and statistical approach was employed by various scientists. One of the first was made by workers in France, who, like Hippocrates, divided people into four physical and mental types, according to their most obvious body part. In this way they distinguished the digestive, the thoracic, the musculo-articular, and the cerebral type of person.

A more recent four-fold division of mankind was outlined by the German psychiatrist Ernst Kretschmer (1888-1964) in his book *Körperbau und Charakter* (Physique and Character), published shortly after the end of the First World War. Kretschmer identified two contrasting types of human physique, the short and plump or *pyknic* person and the tall and thin or *asthenic* person, and two intermediate types, the muscular *athletic* person and the physically mixed or *dysplastic* person, which correspond in a general way to the four types described by Hippocrates.

-------------------- **4** --------------------

If you are below average height and have what is euphemistically called a 'full figure,' that is, short, plump limbs, a fat stomach, and a broad behind, and also a large head and a broad, round face, then you are a pyknic person. Kretschmer claims that such a physical appearance accompanies a generally easy-going, extroverted and optimistic personality, although one that can quickly become depressed, unhappy and pessimistic when things go wrong. He called this up-and-down temperament *cycloid*, and you may have experienced such mood swings yourself. Hence it is not surprising to learn that most manic-depressives have a pyknic physique. Where your physical health is concerned, you are prone to high blood-pressure and to heart and circulatory disorders, and also to cancer. History records that many dictators, such as the Roman emperor Nero, Napoleon Bonaparte, Benito Mussolini, and Francisco Franco, had a pyknic body build, and indeed a short, plump stature appears to be one of the prime motivating factors in human life.

If, on the other hand, you are tall and thin, with a small head and a long, bony face—you may also have a large nose—then you are an asthenic type. Such a physique, maintains Kretschmer, indicates that you are basically introverted, shy and reserved, but because you may have unstable emotions, you are likely to be nervous and easily upset. Indeed, Kretschmer found that the majority of schizophrenics have an asthenic physique. You are happiest doing your own thing; you avoid social situations where possible, and dislike touching others or being touched. You are typically rather anxious and may have trouble sleeping. You are prone to nervous disorders, to tuberculosis and other chest complaints, and to thyroid gland trouble.

However, if you are neither short and fat nor tall and thin, then you will in all probability have either an athletic physique or a mixed dysplastic physique. The typical athletic person is of average height, and has a well-muscled frame, broad shoulders, and narrow hips. The face is large and angular, the jaw strong, and the nose somewhat flattened. If this description fits yourself, your body type reveals that your temperament is very similar to that of the asthenic person, that is, it is *schizoid*. You are therefore something of a loner, and prefer to make your own way in the world. You are quite shy, and easily become upset or nonplussed when things do not go as expected. You tend to suffer from the same health problems as the asthenic type.

The second intermediate type, the dysplastic (from *dys* or 'bad' and *plasia* or 'formation'), is a physical mixture, having elements found in the other three types. However, there may be some primitive features in evidence, such as a small head and face, a low forehead, and a small nose. Thus a tall, obese person and a short, thin person, especially if they have individual body parts that are not fully formed, would fall into the dysplastic category. Kretschmer says that such a physique belongs to the person who is emotionally immature, psychologically out of balance, and rather shiftless and irresponsible. And yet dysplastic people often possess artistic talents and clever minds, so that if you belong to this group you share your features with many famous writers, musicians, poets and artists, like Ernest Hemingway, Pablo Picasso, Salvador Dali, and T.S. Eliot.

An American researcher, W.H. Sheldon, later largely substantiated Kretschmer's findings, yet disagreed with him to the extent of claiming that there were in reality only three, not four, primary physical types, which he identified by terms that have since passed into common usage, the *endomorph*, the *ectomorph*, and the *mesomorph*. The endomorph is distinguished by his or her shortness and stoutness, and therefore corresponds to Kretschmer's pyknic type; the ecto-morph is tall and thin, and thus corresponds to the asthenic type; and the mesomorph is muscular and strong, and hence most closely resembles the athletic type. Moreover, Sheldon differed from Kretschmer by claiming that each of these types has its own temperament, which is linked with the body part that is emphasized. Thus the endomorph is viscero-tonic or social by nature, the ectomorph is cerebrotonic or intellectual, and the mesomorph is somatotonic or physical.

More recently a Beverly Hills, California, physician named Elliot Abravanel has suggested that a person's body type is influenced by the activity of one or other of the four most important ductless or endocrine glands, viz. the thyroid, the adrenals, the pituitary, and the gonads (i.e. the ovaries and the testes), which thereby produce four physical and tem-perament types, whose characteristics may best be described as glandular. You may be able to recognize yourself as a par-ticular gland type from the brief descriptions of each given below.

5

You are a thyroid or T-type, according to Dr Abravanel, if you have a tall, spare frame, fairly wide shoulders, wavy hair, sparkling eyes, and straight teeth. You also tend to speak rapidly, and when you gain weight, the fat accumulates around your middle. However, unlike Kretschmer's asthenic person, whom you most closely resemble, your behaviour is episodic, or potentially manic-depressive, with bursts of activity being followed by periods of withdrawal and depres-sion, due to the fact that the thyroid acts on the brain in a cyclical manner. Many artists and journalists, he says, have this body type and temperament, so you are in good company.

If you have a big-boned, strong yet fleshy body, wide-set eyes, and are balding if you are a man, or have large breasts and a flat bottom if you are a woman, such characteristics identify you as an adrenal or A-type person. The adrenal hormones have their greatest effect on the brain's aggressive centres, which explains why you are short-tempered and argumentative, yet also self-confident and self-assured. You fare well in the business world and in any job or profession that is at all combative. You are also very stubborn, which gives you the ability to stick at tasks until they are completed.

However, if you have a delicate, waif-like appearance, with a large head, match-stick limbs, and fine hair, then you are a pituitary or P-type person. As such, you have a non-physical, intellectual temperament, which equips you for mental pursuits, for learning and investigating, and for arguing and debating. You are also quite creative. You dislike emotional involvement, and you do not have a strong sex drive.

You are a gonadal or G-type person if you are heavier below the waist than above, with a noticeably large bottom, although you are blessed with a flat stomach. When you go on a diet you lose weight steadily and only put it on slowly. You have a pleasant, even disposition, and are caring and helpful. Indeed, you are essentially an intuitive, feeling type, who is happiest looking after others. Female G-types, you may care to note, make the best wives and mothers, secretaries and actresses, and G-types of both sexes are good team-workers.

Dr Abravanel also makes the somewhat odd claim that the endocrinal type of woman (although not, strange to say, of man) can be judged from the food and drink that she most enjoys. If you are a coffee and doughnuts person, this marks you out as a T-type. Should your preferences lie more in the direction of hamburger and chips, they reveal that you are an A-type. If you go bananas over milkshakes, then you are an intellectual P-type, while if cake and biscuits are more your thing—particularly if they are home-baked—you are quite definitely a G-type. If you love all these foods, it presumably means that not only are you endocrinally mixed-up, but that you also have one foot in the grave.

Another way of classifying people with an alphabet letter tag was devised in the early 1970s by two San Francisco cardiologists, Dr Meyer Friedman and Dr Ray Rosenman, whose purpose was altogether more serious. For they had discovered from carrying out a study of 3,500 businessmen, that those who had competitive, angry, hostile and impatient personalities, and who always felt pressed for time, had twice the risk of having a heart attack than their more relaxed and easy-going colleagues. They designated the former as Type-A people and the latter as Type-B people, and in fact it has since been shown that 90 per cent of all heart attack victims are Type-As.

Doctors Friedman and Rosenman did not comment about the physical build of Type-A and Type-B people, but it is evident from the previous descriptions of body type and associated personality, that the Type-A personality has much in common with that of Aristotle's tall, slim and upright man and with the lean, hairy and yellow-complexioned choleric type of Hippocrates. He also shares many of the Mercury and the Mars planetary type characteristics, the former being short and slim, the latter being of average height and thickset. And his aggressiveness matches that of Dr Abravanel's aptly named adrenal or A-type, who is large-boned and balding if male and big-breasted and small-bottomed if a female. We can therefore conclude that if you are either a tall or a short slim person, or if you are a medium-sized, fleshily-built person, you probably have a Type-A personality.

Although Dr Friedman's and Dr Roseman's research was carried out with American businessmen, subsequent studies have shown that women often display Type-A personality characteristics. In fact it has been estimated that 70 per cent of American men and 40-50 per cent of American women show Type-A behaviour. One California psychologist, Harriet B. Braiker, has even suggested that those women who both work and run a home, and who are intent on making a success of both activities, suffer more stress than Type-A men. She therefore designates these women as Type-E— the 'E' presumably standing for 'excessive'—and believes that not only do they run a greater risk of suffering a heart attack, but have their lives made miserable by their constant tiredness, irritability, and despondency, driven as they are by their insatiable desire to succeed.

6

The following check-list will enable you to determine if you display Type-A characteristics. The more traits you have, the greater is your risk of suffering a heart attack before you reach the age of 65. The Type-A person:

1 is impatient;
2 is competitive;
3 is angry, hostile, and cynical;
4 is pressed for time;
5 is unable to relax;
6 walks, talks and eats quickly;
7 needs to get things done fast;
8 schedules more work and play into less time;
9 does not listen to what other people say;
10 is insensitive to the beauty of nature and that of his surroundings.

Unfortunately, Type-A people believe that their hurry-hurry, rush-rush approach to their work makes them more efficient, more capable, and thus somehow superior to others, but in fact the opposite is true, as they tend to make more mistakes, produce late and often slovenly results, and have constant altercations with their fellows. They are also involved in more car accidents and have less happy and satisfying marriages than those with a quieter and more patient Type-B personality. And they often drink and smoke heavily. Then why do they behave as they do? The reason, according to psychologists, is that Type-A behaviour stems from a negative self-image and a low self-esteem, which encourages them to compensate for their supposed deficiencies by challenging all and winning whenever possible. They need, however, to step off the treadmill that they have created for themselves, if they are to save their lives and preserve their sanity. Hence it is fortunate to know that a Type-A person can convert himself into a Type-B, and in so doing both improve his self-esteem and lower his risk of having a heart attack, by following the tips given below, all of which will encourage him to slow down and enjoy life. What he (or you) must do is:

1 get to know more Type-B people;
2 not hog conversations. Listen to others when they talk, don't finish their sentences for them, and don't hurry them along with such interjections as 'I see, I see' and 'Yes, yes';
3 stop making appointments at a definite time;
4 keep your desk or workplace tidy;
5 employ a Type-B secretary or try to work with Type-B people;
6 eat lunch alone or with those who don't talk shop;
7 be big enough to admit that you can't achieve all your goals;
8 tell yourself that even God took a rest after creating the world;
9 write out and hang up the saying 'Make haste slowly' where you can easily see it;
10 ask yourself, when confronted with a pressing assignment, if it will be important in five years' time.

Chapter Two
THE OPEN FACE

I know the thing that's most uncommon;
(Envy, be silent, and attend!)
I know a reasonable Woman,
Handsome and witty, yet a Friend.

We are known by our faces, whose features are more familiar to us than any other part of our bodies. Yet this was not always so. In the distant past, before the invention of mirrors, a person rarely saw his (or her) own face, which was therefore something of a mystery to him. And this explains why the divinely handsome Narcissus became captivated by his reflection when he happened to catch sight of it in the quiet waters of a spring. The poor youth promptly fell in love with himself, but being denied love's consummation, stabbed himself to death.

But nowadays every home has its own mirror or mirrors, and reflective surfaces of all sorts, such as shop windows, show us our faces, should we care to look at them, at every turn.

I look into my glass
And view my wasted skin,
And say, 'Would God it came to pass
My heart had shrunk as thin.'

So wrote the aged Thomas Hardy, who was clearly not averse to viewing his reflection, even though he was not entirely pleased by what he saw. But some people, surprisingly enough, avoid looking at themselves, while others cannot pass a mirror without checking themselves out. Indeed, the frequency with which you do just that can be very revealing.

7

Psychologists say that if you usually or always gaze at yourself in a mirror or other reflective surface that you happen to come across, perhaps stopping to make some small adjustment to your hair or dress as you do so, it indicates that your self-esteem is low, that you are insecure, and that you may feel unwanted and unloved. Thus your too frequent appraisal of yourself means that you are constantly worried that you might look as bad as you feel.

Yet if you make a point of never looking in a mirror, this also reveals that you are not very well adjusted. After all, we all need to check ourselves out in a mirror once or twice a day, in order to make sure we are presentable. But if you avoid doing so, it suggests that you are in conflict with society, as you do not wish to conform to its standards. You may also be a somewhat aggressive person who resents authority and who feels that by refusing to look at yourself you are thumbing your nose at the world.

Both types of behaviour reflect inner disquiet, the first stemming from inferiority and the second from a misguided superiority. Hence if you observe your reflection only occasionally, you can take comfort from your actions.

We all know that our facial expressions divulge our inner mood, and indeed it is chiefly through our face that we communicate our feelings to others. Drooping shoulders and a bowed head also give out a message, as does a more upright and alert stance, but these postures only reinforce what the face says, although as we shall shortly discover, they too can be very revealing.

It is interesting to note, however, that while our mood does create our expression, the opposite is apparently also true, that our expressions can influence our moods. This quite amazing, and potentially very useful and important, observation was reported in 1907 by Israel Waynbaum in his book *Physionomie humaine: son mécanisme et son rôle social*. He suggests that a particular expression modifies the blood flow to the brain and in so doing alters its neurochemistry, which in turn creates the subjective state that normally accompanies the expression. This means, for example, that if you want to feel happy, all you have to do is smile. In fact why not try smiling now? Pull a big one. Hold it. Don't you feel your mood improving? Of course you do. And that's what they used to call the secret of happiness.

But while expressions are important in revealing mood, our faces can tell much more about us than that. Indeed, physiognomists claim that our characters and dispositions, even our fates, can be read in the shape and the lineaments of our faces. I myself believe this to be true, and I have written a book about face-reading that the interested reader may care to consult (*How to Read Faces*, The Aquarian Press 1989). Here we have space to note only some of the more recently discovered clues to character that are shown by the face.

You may have noticed that the two halves of your face are not identical. One of your ears or eyes or eyebrows, for example, may be larger or more protruding or higher set than the other, which disrupts the symmetry of your face. In fact this is why many film actors or actresses will only show one profile, their best, to the camera. It is also true that we can be classified as 'right-faced' or 'left-faced' according to the amount of movement which takes place on one side of the face or the other when we talk. And this in turn says something about how we use our brains.

8

If you watch someone's face when he (or she) talks to you, it will be noticed that there is more movement on one side than the other. For instance, the person concerned may raise his right eyebrow in preference to the left, or may turn his head more often to the right, or may twitch the right side of his face more than the left, etc., or do all these things. Or, conversely, the movements may be concentrated on the left side. The former person, according to Dr Karl Smith, a psychologist at the University of Wisconsin, is right-faced, and the latter left-faced. In his study of the facial movements made by students, Dr Smith found that 88 per cent of them were right-faced.

Now it is an odd fact about the brain that its left half or hemisphere controls the right side of the body, while its right hemisphere directs the left side of the body. Thus a right-faced person is making more use of the left half of his brain, which can be considered the dominant hemisphere, whereas a left-faced person is doing the opposite: he has a dominant right hemisphere. And once we know that, we also know a good deal about how he or she thinks.

This is because the right hemisphere is mainly concerned with non-verbal activities, such as spatial orientation, face and object recognition, creative thought, imagery, and the recognition of melodies, while the left hemisphere is responsible for speech and writing skills, and for analytical and abstract thought. Left-faced people therefore tend to be more artistic and musical than right-faced people, who by and large are logical, verbal types. Left-faced people are also more independent and unconventional than the right-faced. Hence we should not be surprised by Karl Smith's discovery that musicians are invariably left-faced.

9

A quicker way of determining whether a person has a dominant right hemisphere or left hemisphere is to ask him (or her) a question that requires some concentrated thought (such as multiplying two figures together), and noting the direction in which he looks, or shifts his eyes, when considering the problem. The shifting of the gaze is automatic, and occurs when the attention is switched from outside matters to inside concerns. Some people, the majority in fact, glance to the right, while others look to the left. Because studies have shown that when one side of the brain is electrically stimulated the eyes move in the opposite direction, this means that the former have a dominant left hemisphere and the latter a dominant right hemisphere. Hardly surprisingly, in another study involving students, it was found that those taking courses in philosophy and science, which are subjects requiring logic and analysis, tended to shift their eyes to the right, whereas those studying the humanities glanced predominantly to the left.

Brain hemisphere dominance is also revealed by left-handedness and right-handedness, although it is not always immediately obvious where others are concerned which hand is favoured for writing, etc. Left-handedness and right-handedness are considered in the next chapter.

The eyes also reveal much information about the personality by their colour. Among animals, it was long ago noticed that those with dark-coloured eyes, such as eagles, kingfishers, bats, otters, dogs, weasels, wolves, and wolverines, have a rapid reaction 'attack or flee' behaviour pattern, whereas those with light-coloured eyes, like herons, grebes, wild cats, leopards, tigers, lions, jaguars, ocelots, and foxes, are far more cautious, employing as they do a 'watch and stalk' approach, both hunting and escaping by stealth. And it has since been shown that similar behavioural differences are found among people with dark-coloured and light-coloured irises.

10

If your irises are brown or black, although black eyes are very rare, you have dark-coloured eyes. If they are blue or green, or light grey, you have light-coloured eyes, even though the depth of shade of blue and green eyes can vary quite considerably. Should you have hazel eyes, then you are classified as having eyes of an intermediate colour.

If you belong to the first group, your dark irises reveal that you have quick reactions, that you respond rapidly to sudden events, that you are easily shocked or upset, and that you function best when you are under pressure. You are also rather impatient, have a short temper, and are blessed with plenty of energy. You have a short concentration span, mainly because you are easily distracted by things going on around you.

However, your personality is rather different if you have light-coloured eyes. For a start, you hate having to make quick decisions, thus you like to listen and consider, and are overall more cautious and thoughtful. In fact you do not function very well if you are pushed for time or are otherwise under pressure, although you have excellent staying power and perseverance if you can work at your own pace. And because you are a good listener, you are more suited to those professions that require sustained and sympathetic attention, such as marriage guidance and psychiatry, than those with dark eyes.

It has been shown that dark-eyed people tend to prefer, and do best at, those sports, like rugby and football, which are active and which require quick reactions, and those roles, like batting in cricket, which call for speed of response. People with light-coloured eyes, on the other hand, have a greater propensity for sports like golf and snooker, games like chess and bridge, and those activities such as bowling in cricket, which require considered thought and strategy.

The hazel-eyed fall somewhere between these two personality extremes, being neither as testy and impatient as the dark-eyed nor as slow and conservative as the light-eyed. Hence if you survey the world with a pair of fine hazel eyes, then you should in theory be happier and better adjusted than your dark- and light-eyed cousins. So chalk one up to yourself, you lucky dog!

The way in which people hold or move their eyes can often reveal if they are lying. Care is needed in this regard, however, as cultural differences must be taken into account. We in the West, for example, prefer others to look directly at us when they are speaking, which we usually interpret as a sign of their honesty, whereas in many Eastern countries, it is a mark of respect to lower one's gaze when addressing another, especially if he or she has a higher status. The typical Easterner regards the direct gaze as both an expression of insolence and dishonesty.

However, while there are certain clues which suggest that an untruth has been told, there is as yet no foolproof method of lie-detection, chiefly because ordinary nervousness, which is known to particularly affect shy people, produces many of the tell-tale signs that are displayed by the liar. This is why looking away while talking, or covering the mouth, or fidgeting, all of which are popularly associated with lying, may simply be nervous reactions, and thus entirely innocent.

Yet when someone tells a deliberate lie, it is usually accompanied by specific bodily—often facial—signs, which are generated by the heightened emotion that the liar experiences. But such signs are far less apparent when the lie is pre-planned, or when the liar is used to telling untruths, although Paul Ekman, a psychologist at the University of California at San Francisco, says, 'Lying is a special talent, not easily acquired. One must be a natural performer, winning and charming in manner.'

It was Dr Ekman and his colleagues who discovered, by making a careful examination of a videotaped interview with 'Mary', a suicidal psychiatric patient who lied about her negative, self-destructive feelings, that her face showed many extremely brief 'micro-expressions', which betrayed how she really felt. For example, she would let a flash of despair cross her face before hiding this with a false smile. Indeed, the discovery of micro-expressions such as these, along with other evidence, suggests that it is harder to lie about feelings than about facts.

11

The following are believed by psychologists to be the most reliable signs that a person is lying:

1   The pupils of the eyes dilate.
2   The eyelids close, or the rate of blinking increases.
3   The voice pitch becomes higher.
4   The speech rate increases, as does its volume.
5   Sweat appears on the forehead, or elsewhere on the face.
6   The breathing becomes faster and shallower.
7   The lips tighten to hide most of their bulk.
8   There is a lack of animation in the face, voice and body.
9   There is a longer than normal delay in answering questions—e.g. 'With whom did you have lunch today, dear?'—that should produce an immediate response.
10 There is more hesitation, suggested by such interjections as 'ah', 'um', and 'you know'.
11 The expressions last 5 to 10 seconds.
12 The appearance of micro-expressions which contrast with the overall expression, suggesting that it is feigned.
13 A smile that does not employ the muscles around the eyes, or a look of sadness that does not involve the forehead, reveal feigned feelings.
14 The muscles contract more tightly on one side of the face than on the other, giving it a lop-sided look.
15 Fewer body gestures, such as nodding, chin tilting and hand waving.
16 The appearance of untypical body gestures, such as touching the face or pulling at the hair.

Some liars also give themselves away by unconsciously showing delight when they think that they have fooled you, and also by visibly relaxing when the lie has been told.

However, although each of these visual or auditory signs

may reveal a lie, Dr Ekman warns: 'A lie catcher should never rely on one clue to deceit. There must be many. The facial clues should be confirmed by clues from voice, words, or body.'

The next time you look through your photograph album, or that belonging to someone else, make a note of how you or they pose when the camera clicks. The stance adopted at this important time shows how you and others feel about yourselves.

12

Back in 1973, two academics at Cambridge University—Dr I.C. McManus and Dr N.K. Humphrey—examined portraits of members of the English and European royal houses and the landed gentry from the eighteenth to the twentieth century, and found that the majority of those represented had turned the left side of their faces towards the artist or camera. This suggests, they concluded, that those modern, non-aristocratic people who present their left cheek to the camera are unconsciously revealing that they think they are rather special—superior types, in fact. Hence if you do this, you have a high opinion of yourself. But if, on the other hand, you display your right profile or gaze full-faced into the camera, then your opinion of yourself is more modest.

Now, where your looks are concerned, how do you rate? Are you in the Venus or the Adonis category? Or is your face (and figure) less pleasing to the eye? Or could you be ugly? Your appearance is important, not only because your looks affect how others react to you, but because your success in life is related to how ugly or good-looking you are. But first, check which of these categories you belong to: (1) strikingly handsome or beautiful; (2) above average; (3) average; (4) below average; or (5) ugly. Then read on.

13

If your looks are above average or better, you live in a different world from everybody else—or so says Michael Hughes,
who is a sociologist at Virginia Polytechnic and State University. 'People who are attractive', he claims, 'elicit different
responses from their environment. People automatically
attribute competency to you, they automatically think you're
smarter.'

In a study conducted with colleague Debra Umberson,
Hughes interviewed 3,600 people and rated their looks. Of
the sample 3 per cent were striking, 30.6 per cent were above
average, 54.9 per cent were average, 9.7 per cent were below
average, and 1.8 per cent were unattractive. Those who had
above average or superior looks were found to be both better educated and to earn a higher income than those belonging to other categories. And when Hughes and Umberson
took all relevant factors into consideration, such as age, sex,
marriage, income, and occupation, the better-looking
reported more life satisfaction than their less attractive fellows. However, when good-looking people with a lower
educational standard were compared with equivalently educated homely types, they were found to have gained no
advantages in life, but as the level of education increased,
the better-looking were employed in more prestigious jobs
and made more money. And significantly, good-looking men
and women did equally well for themselves.

But if you feel that you are below average in looks, don't
despair, as another American study shows that the Venuses
and the Adonises don't have everything their own way. In
fact researchers Richard Urdy and Bruce Eckland at the
University of North Carolina found that when it comes to
getting ahead in life it is the uglies who are laughing all the
way to the bank. Ugly men, that is. Beautiful women still
hold most of the cards.

'There is significant evidence that female attractiveness
affects her adult status through marriage to a high income
husband,' they report. In other words, if you are a beauti-

ful woman, even though you might not be very well educated, you stand an above-average chance of marrying a well-off or powerful man.

It is only the outstandingly handsome men, according to Urdy and Eckland, who gain from their looks by obtaining prestigious jobs. Men who are merely good-looking tend to do less well at school, marry earlier, and take jobs with little status.

Homely-looking or ugly men, however, often compensate for their unattractiveness by becoming better educated and by working harder, which eventually not only brings them a high paying job and greater social status, but often a good-looking, clever wife.

But why do these two studies come to different conclusions with regard to good-looking, yet not outstandingly good-looking, men? This can probably be explained by age differences. The 601 men and the 745 women in the Urdy and Eckland study were all middle-aged and had thus attended school and college in the 1950s and 1960s, when attitudes towards education and jobs were conditioned by the labour shortage of the time, whereas the people in the study conducted by Hughes and Umberson came from a variety of age groups, which meant that many had been at school and college since the economic squeeze of 1973-4, when the job market contracted and attitudes to education and employment underwent a sea change. Pretty boys woke up to the fact that the world is a tough place and that they could not get by on their looks alone, but that, once educated, the world was at their feet.

Paying attention to body language—the way emotions and feelings are revealed by the stance and by the way in which the different body parts are held and positioned—became popular in the 1970s, when several books were written about it. While body language can never be an exact science, as factors other than a person's inner state can affect his or her posture, it can be very revealing when used circumspectly.

Below are some of the messages that can be read from the head and face.

14

When the person to whom you are speaking maintains eye contact, it means that he (or she) is interested in what you are saying and is receptive to its content. It can also reveal understanding. But when the listener averts his eyes, it usually means that he is uninterested in what you are saying or lacks enthusiasm for your ideas. However, failure to engage in eye contact can also be caused by shyness or nervousness. Eyes that are held widely open, when not registering momentary surprise, also normally signify interest and alertness, but they can sometimes reveal puzzlement and thoughtfulness. Staring eyes, by contrast, are generally a sign of hostility and aggression. Yet in certain circumstances staring eyes indicate a great interest.

A mouth that smiles is usually welcoming, and so signifies interest, openness, and friendliness. But to be genuine, the smile must involve other parts of the face, particularly the muscles around the eyes. A non-smiling, tight mouth is one sign of disapproval, even anger, while a frowning mouth registers either doubt or thoughtfulness, or displeasure. Lips that tighten together so as to hide their red, fleshy portion, suggest that a lie has been told.

When the head is held upright, it reflects positive inner feelings, like confidence, interest and alertness, whereas a drooping head is a mark of dismay, sadness or withdrawal. A cocked head can show suspicion, although it usually indicates curiosity and interest.

The wearing of hats has now largely gone out of fashion, yet for those few who still wear one, as does the author, it is worth bearing in mind Lord Baden-Powell's observation, recorded in *Scouting for Boys*, that the placement of a hat on the head reveals character.

15

'If it is worn slightly on one side,' he writes, 'the wearer is good natured; if it is worn very much on one side, he is a swaggerer; if on the back of his head, he is bad at paying his debts; if worn straight on top, he is probably honest, but very dull.'

Moustaches are more commonly met with than hats in modern life, although beards have slumped in popularity since their 'with-it' peak of the 1960s. Moustaches may seem to be respectable and innocent, but their presence is psychologically very revealing. Indeed, it was author Ian Fleming, an astute observer of human behaviour, who advised: 'Beware of people who smell, and tread carefully in the company of moustaches, sideburns and beards.'

16

If you have a moustache you may feel that it improves your appearance, by making you more handsome or dignified, or that it enhances your masculinity. Yet according to Dr Neville Parker, an Australian psychiatrist, the real reason is quite different. For following a two-year study of the Australian male, he has concluded that 99 per cent of men who wear moustaches are suffering from emotional, particularly sexual, problems. And Dr Parker says that the smaller the moustache, the larger the feeling of personal inadequacy that it symbolizes. Men with large, bushy moustaches, by contrast, are less likely to suffer from sexual difficulties, although they do tend to be obsessional types. The bushy-moustachioed typically engage in the same activities year after year, yet derive little satisfaction from what they are doing.

Many people have one or more nervous habits which they find embarrassing and would like to stop. Most of these

involve the head or face, the commonest being (1) over-
eating; (2) chain-smoking; (3) nail-biting; (4) eye-blinking;
(5) lisping; (6) muscle-twitching; (7) stuttering; (8) thumb-
sucking; (9) hair-twisting; (10) tongue-thrusting; (11)
nervous-coughing; (12) gum-sucking; (13) head-scratching;
(14) head-shaking or -jerking, and (15) pencil-chewing. But
there is another that is both annoying to others and potentially disfiguring, which people often do when they are
asleep and thus may not be aware of it, namely tooth-
grinding or bruxism. It can result in the wearing away of
tooth enamel, and there are cases on record where the teeth
have been ground down to the gums. You may be a bruxist. But if so, what does it say about you?

17

Like most other nervous habits, bruxism has an emotional
cause. In fact a 1972 study found that many tooth-grinders
are, or had been, bed-wetters, nail-biters, or pencil-chewers.
The association between bruxism and nail-biting and pencil-
chewing is not surprising, as each is substituting for the urge
to bite, destroy and devour that which is troubling the person concerned. Thus your tooth grinding is a symptom of
pent-up hostility and anger. Such inner tension may be
caused by working in a job with a tight deadline, like newspaper reporting, or you may be engaged in exacting preci-
sion work, such as watchmaking or repairing, computer
assembling, gemstone grinding, or even typing.

Another study, conducted in 1976 by researchers at
Fairleigh Dickinson University, reported that many bruxists
are women, and that these were 'perfectionists who have
a tendency to become anxious and depressed.' They are typically married to docile and passive men.

If you are a bruxist it goes without saying that if you want
to give up your habit, you need to pinpoint exactly what
it is that is raising your blood pressure, and find a way of
removing or circumventing the difficulty before you ruin
your teeth. If you suspect that you might be a bruxist but

are not sure, your dentist will be able to tell you if your teeth show signs of abnormal wear.

Eating and lovemaking have long been linked, and not only because the former is often a prelude to the latter. The two are alike in that both involve oral activity: the lips, after all, are erogenous zones, and a lover grazes upon his beloved's lips with perhaps more enthusiasm than he might slurp an ice cream. It is not surprising, therefore, that some psychologists maintain the connection between eating and lovemaking is so close that a person's food preferences, and his (or her) eating habits, reflect his more intimate interests and capabilities. This gives a new and fresh meaning to the old adage, 'You are what you eat.'

18

If you enjoy your food and like tucking into a good meal, then you probably enjoy sex. This is because eating and sex are both pleasurable, life-enhancing activities, and an enjoyment of the first shows that you do not feel guilty about taking the time to please yourself. But if you pick at your food and never seem to have any appetite, it means that you don't have much interest in, or energy for, sex. You probably avoid pleasure either because it conflicts with your basic belief that life is meant to be hard or because you think it is wrong.

19

Next, ask yourself if you nibble at your food, biting off small pieces that require little, if any, chewing, or do you take in fair-sized mouthfuls that you enjoy chewing? In other words, are you a biter or a chewer?

If you are a biter you are probably quite an anxious person, who finds it difficult to relax and enjoy sex. You thus prefer your lovemaking activities to be brief and infrequent. But if you chew your food—although not necessarily 30 times—this signifies that you are a calmer and more sensual type, which means that you like to make love often and enjoy taking your time over it.

20

Imagine that you have gone into a sandwich bar for lunch, and that there are four types of sandwich on sale: salmon, prawn, roast beef, and chicken. Which one of these would be your choice?

Salmon fanciers, according to a recent study, are rather like the fish of their choosing, which always returns to the same stream to breed. Hence if you are a salmon sandwich person, you are an enthusiastic, active lover, but you are not promiscuous and you prefer to make love in familiar surroundings. And you don't mind making a special effort to please.

Prawn-fanciers tend to be ambitious, go-getting types, whose energies carry over into the bedroom. If therefore you would pick a prawn sandwich, you are probably a demanding and passionate bed partner, although you seldom lose your heart and you are by no means monogamous. Indeed, you may believe that where sex is concerned, variety is the spice of life.

Roast beef lovers, surprisingly enough, are brain people, who are more interested in ideas and mental games than in fleshy gropings. Thus if you would select a roast beef sandwich, you are not likely to be a hot-blooded lover or even someone who thinks much about sex. However, once you are between the sheets, you do your best to please your partner.

Chicken-choosers are not the brightest of people, but they do have big hearts and warm natures. If your hand would go out to the chicken sandwiches, it means that not only do you like to touch and cuddle, but when you are in bed with your lover or spouse you enjoy both giving and receiving pleasure. You are also a faithful type, so that you won't cross the road unless your lover lets you down.

21

Are you a fast eater or do you like to masticate your food well before sending it below? And do you take an interest and perhaps a special pleasure in what's on your plate?—or don't you much care what it is as long as it's edible?

The answers to these questions are important, because according to Guy's Hospital psychologist Maurice Yaffé, who interviewed female volunteers about their partner's eating and lovemaking habits, there is a direct correlation—if you're a man—between the speed at which you eat and the interest you take in your food, and your ability as a lover.

If you are a slow, careful eater with an interest in food, you belong to the superior lover category. Those women with partners who chewed slowly and who took an interest in what they were eating, said that their men were warm, sensual and sensitive lovers.

However, if you are a slow eater but have little interest in the food itself, then you are likely to have problems in both obtaining and sustaining an erection.

Should you be a faster eater yet at the same time take an interest in food, this signifies that you are an anxious bed partner, with whom women find it difficult to relax. You may also suffer from premature ejaculation.

If you are a fast eater who lacks any interest in food, then you are not very interested in sex. Thus your sex life is likely to be either very low key or non-existent.

Indeed, Maurice Yaffé discovered that four types of people comprise this last group: (1) those who are sexually immature and have no sex at all; (2) those who have a low sex drive and who are sexually celibate; (3) those who substitute food for sex and who therefore tend to be overweight, and (4) those who are unable to ejaculate and who find it difficult to get emotionally involved with their partner(s).

Lastly, you may be interested to know that your mood and your work efficiency may depend upon what you had for breakfast. According to Dr Richard Wurtman, an endocrinologist at the Massachussetts Institute of Technology, your breakfast menu 'can affect the brain and, subsequently, the way you think and feel throughout the day. Every study we've seen thus far shows that eating carbohydrates, whether sugar or starch, tends to make people less active and more calm and sleepy.' A high protein meal, such as bacon and eggs, on the other hand, has the opposite effect.

Chapter Three
THE REVEALING HANDS

All are but parts of one stupendous whole,
Whose body Nature is, and God the Soul.

Apart from our faces and our figures, the hands are the most readily recognizable parts of our bodies. To the individual, who is looking out at the world and whose view of himself is necessarily limited, his hands are probably more familiar to him than the rest of his body. In fact because your hands are unique to yourself, they must symbolize yourself, and if they can be interpreted they can therefore reveal your nature. This is why we shall be examining how the hands can be read in this chapter.

If this perhaps sends a shudder through you, let me hasten to add that we are not going to discuss the meanings of the lines of the hands, but rather how the hands are used, their morphology, and the significance of rings and wrist-watches. These are areas which have all been investigated by psychologists and other scientists, and they have the advantage from our point of view of being more readily visible in the hands of others. Hence without needing to stray into a study—palmistry—that many regard as superstitious nonsense (although I don't believe that it is), we can learn a good deal about others, and you about yourself, by taking note of the meanings of the hand features dealt with below.

The condition of one's hands discloses, in a general sense, one's work. Hands that bear calluses, have split nails, and

The condition of one's hands discloses, in a general sense, one's work. Hands that bear calluses, have split nails, and are begrimed with dirt, suggest a manual occupation, whereas those that are smooth and clean indicate a more cerebral type of job. But while this is interesting enough by itself, it is more helpful where character is concerned to pay attention to those traits that directly reflect it, such as the colour of the hands, their size and shape, their dryness or moistness, the condition of their nails, and the length and thickness of the fingers. Fingerprint patterns are also important in this sense, although they cannot be seen in another without his or her active participation.

We shall first examine the different hand shapes, as these can, give an insight into character and personality. Like the body, the hands can be classified according to two different systems. The first, which was devised by a nineteenth-century French army officer named C.S. D'Arpentigny, identifies seven basic hand shapes, and thus accords in a general way with the seven body types remarked upon by Aristotle. The second, following the system outlined by Hippocrates, recognizes four different types of hand, each of which is named after one of the four ancient elements: Earth, Water, Fire, and Air. These form a loose parallel with the four body types described by Ernst Kretschmer.

22

The seven hand shapes of D'Arpentigny are known respectively as (1) elementary; (2) spatulate; (3) square; (4) conical; (5) philosophical; (6) psychical; and (7) mixed. They can be recognized by their size and overall appearance, by the length and shape of their fingers, and by the shape of their nails. Each symbolizes a particular set of character traits and an associated personality type.

(1) *The elementary hand*: this is typically a coarse, strong and stoutly-fashioned hand, with a large, square palm and short, stiff fingers. The fingernails are small and short. As the name suggests, this hand type betokens the sim-

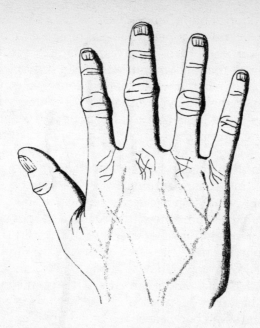

Figure 7: The elementary hand

ple, unsophisticated person, who, while often possessing plenty of energy and animal vigour, has a limited intellect and understanding. If you have elementary hands, then you are an artless, rather dull individual, who prefers to lead an undemanding, yet structured existence. You like physical work that is repetitious and uncomplicated. You have a strong sex drive and a short temper, a combination that can get you into trouble if you're not careful.

(2) *The spatulate hand*: this is a medium-to-large hand, which often displays irregularities like bent fingers. Its characteristic feature is the broadening of the fingertips into a spatulate shape. This shape is sometimes evident in the palms, which may either be broad across the top and narrower across the bottom, or the reverse.

Spatulate hands belong to people who are basically self-reliant individualists, who like to make their own way in

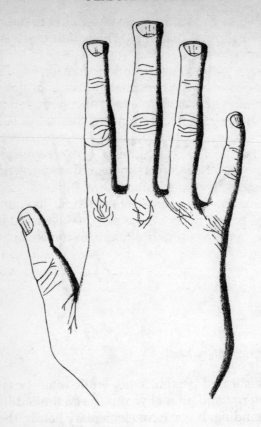

Figure 8: The spatulate hand

the world and who hate to be tied down or restricted. Hence if you have such hands, you won't be happy unless you are either in business for yourself or work at a job that lets you do your own thing. You have plenty of energy and enthusiasm—and ambitions that you want to fulfil. You function best when you are under pressure or when you are starting a new project. Because you dislike routine, you find it difficult to cope with those day-to-day activities that are part of any established business, which you will ideally need to hand over to others. You love to travel, and you tend to get depressed if you are obliged to remain in one place.

(3) *The square hand*: this is a large hand, firm to the touch, with a square palm and fingertips with square ends. A practical, no-nonsense hand.

The square hand belongs to the person whose disposition is the opposite of that described for the spatulate hand type. Here there is suspicion instead of openness, self-control rather than enthusiasm, and a love of the status quo, not a desire for change. Thus if you are the owner of square hands, you are likely to be an orderly, conservative person, who is happiest with what you know and understand. You keep your emotions under control, avoid excess, and look back with longing to past times when people, in your opinion, behaved properly. You are a slow, yet logical thinker, and you have no time for radical views or foolish activities. But while you are normally placed and easy-going, your temper is explosive if you are pushed too far, although you seldom bear a grudge.

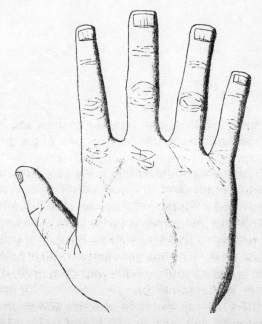

Figure 9: The square hand

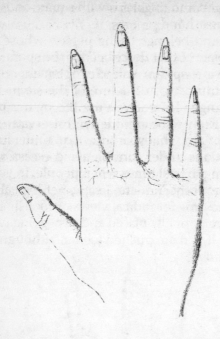

Figure 10: The conical hand

(4) *The conical hand*: this hand type is less thick and heavy, and more graceful in appearance, than any of the preceding hand shapes. In fact it is a small, rather narrow hand, with smooth, unknotted fingers that are conical in form, the fingertips being pointed.

The conical hand belongs to the person who is bright and excitable, eager and interested, yet who lacks sufficient confidence and resolve to achieve much for himself. If you have hands of this type, you are somewhat selfish and self-centred, concerned as you are with your own interests and pleasures, yet at the same time too easily influenced by others in matters of taste. You have an active and quite clever mind, but because you are impulsive and lacking in concentration, you find it almost impossible to stick at anything for long. But despite these faults, you are cheerful and good-humoured, tolerant of the foibles of others, and always willing to listen to another's problems, if only because you like to gossip.

(5) *The philosophical hand*: this is a large, bony hand with long fingers and prominent knuckles. The fingertips are either square or conical, or a mixture of these two shapes.

The philosophical hand denotes a thinking or investigative mind, and thus the person who is critical, sceptical, and reluctant to accept any notion or idea that is unsupported by firm evidence. If you have such hands, you are a fair person, although not particularly warm and welcoming, who keeps your own counsel and who jealously maintains your

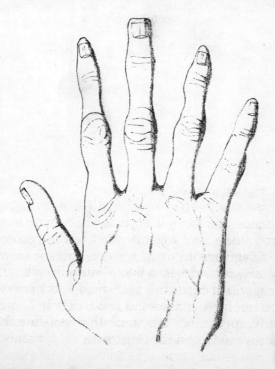

Figure 11: The philosophical hand

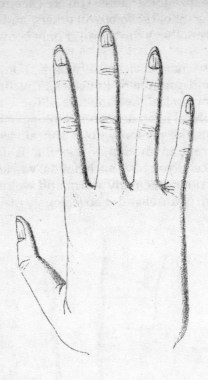

Figure 12: The psychical hand

independence. You love getting to the bottom of things, and indeed your ideas and activities are likely to become more eccentric as you age. In many respects you are a loner, and you may, at worst, develop into a misanthrope.

(6) *The psychical hand*: this is a small and narrow hand, wherein it resembles the conical hand, delicately made and of attractive appearance. The smooth fingers are the same length as the palm, and the fingernails are typically filbert-shaped.

The psychical hand belongs to the rather vague and unrealistic person, whose head is full of other-worldly ideas but whose practical abilities are inadequate for their realization. If you have hands of this type, you are something of a lost soul, unequipped to deal with the demands of life and thus dependent upon others to help you achieve your goals. Yet you are not quite as helpless as you seem, as you often prefer to let those who are willing do what you would rather not do. You have a good intuition, and you could make a passable medium or occultist.

(7) *The mixed hand*: this hand shows, as the name suggests, a mixture of the features that denote the other hand types, which makes it difficult to describe owing to its variability. However, there is characteristically a mixture of fingertip types, the four main ones being the square, the spatulate, the conical and the filbert.

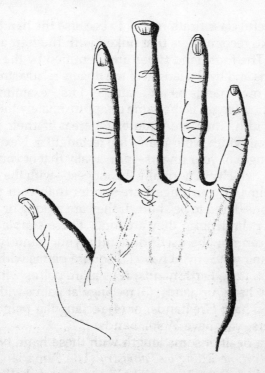

Figure 13: The mixed hand

The mixed hand symbolizes a more complex and rounded person, who possesses character elements found in each of the previously mentioned types. Hence if you have hands of this sort, you are less easy to classify and to pin down. You are likely to function quite well on a variety of levels, having as you probably do an open mind, wide interests, and a modicum of staying power. Yet you may find that you are disadvantaged by your changeability and by your indecision. In this respect you may become a dilettante, tasting and experiencing much but spreading yourself too thinly to become a success in any one field. You may therefore become the victim of disillusion and regret in later life.

A more useful classification, if only because the hand types are easier to recognize, is that linked with the four ancient elements. The four hand types are identified by the shape of the palms and by the length of the fingers relative to them. Take your own hands as an example. First, examine your palms. If their length is the same or approximately the same as their width, they are square, whereas if their length exceeds their width, your palms are rectangular. Next, compare the length of your fingers—principally that of your middle fingers, which are normally the longest—with the length of your palms. If your fingers are shorter than your palms, they are considered to be short. If they are as long or longer than your palm length, they are long. These simple measurements can now be used to identify your hand type, in the following way: If you have (1) square palms with short fingers, you have Earth hands; (2) square palms with long fingers, you have Air hands; (3) rectangular palms with short fingers, you have Fire hands; or (4) rectangular palms with long fingers, you have Water hands.

As I have dealt at some length with these hand types in my book *Fortune-Telling by Palmistry* (The Aquarian Press, 1987), to which the reader might like to refer, I shall simply outline the personality characteristics associated with them here.

_____ **23** _____

(1) Should you have Earth hands, your character and personality is essentially the same as that described for the square hand type mentioned above. That is, you are a placid, moderate, easy-going sort of person, who is practical and down-to-earth and who has fairly fixed views and ideas. You like working outdoors, and you are most comfortable in familiar surroundings with people you know. Although you are slow thinking and rather dull, you may possess artistic talents of a high order. You are slow to anger, yet when you are pushed too far your wrath is explosive.

(2) If you have Air hands, their shape identifies you as a thinking type, which means that you enjoy using your

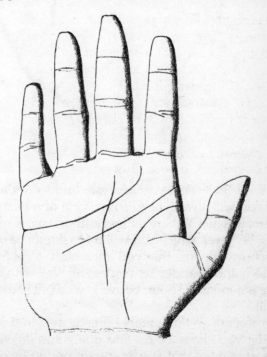

Figure 14: The Earth hand

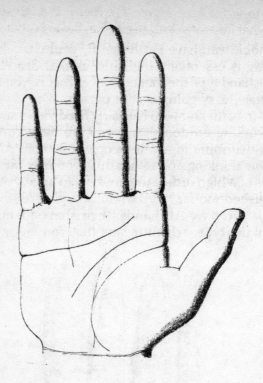

Figure 15: The Air hand

mind—to investigate, to analyse, and to understand—and that you will always need some form of mental stimulation to remain sane. You are far less enthusiastic about your emotions, however, which you will try to dominate or deny. Such self-control means that you are a bit of a cold fish, lacking warmth and sparkle. Yet you get on well with others when there is a mental rapport between you, but badly when there is not.

(3) You are an outgoing, energetic person if you have Fire hands: you like to be up and doing and enjoying life. You are fortunate in that you are rarely put off by obstacles and difficulties, which in fact can stimulate you into trying even harder. You have set goals and ambitions, and you are pre-

pared to work hard to achieve them. But because you are somewhat impatient and dislike having to bother with details or day-to-day routine, you function best as an initiator, handing over to others once the groundwork is done. You are optimistic and enthusiastic, your two most positive traits, and you like to laugh.

(4) If you have Water hands, their form marks you out as a rather dreamy individual, who is shy and introverted, and lacking in confidence. Thus you will need a lot of support, guidance and encouragement if you are to make much of your life. Your acute sensitivity means that you are easily hurt and discouraged, although it gives you an empathy

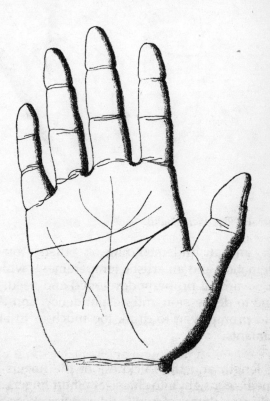

Figure 16: The Fire hand

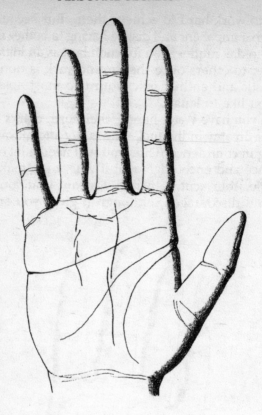

Figure 17: The Water hand

with, and an understanding of, others. You have a rich imagination and an artistic temperament, which can bring you rewards if properly developed and used. But you are prone to depression and despondency, and these in turn could prompt you to drink too much or to take chemical stimulants.

The length and the thickness of the fingers can give an immediate insight into character. Short fingers, for example, betoken quickness of mind and impulsiveness of action, and hence the person who is restless, impatient and keen to be

up and doing, while long fingers belong to the more thoughtful, steady, and cautious individual, who needs to think and
reflect before committing himself to a course of action. Short-
fingered people are therefore spontaneous, feeling types,
whereas long-fingered people are more self-contained and
intellectual. However, the girth of the fingers must also be
taken into consideration, as thick or thin fingers will modify
the above interpretations. Thick fingers are a sign of selfishness and a lack of refinement, and those with them are
thus often brash and rather coarse. Thin fingers, by contrast,
are symbolic of vanity, indecision, and a love of intrigue,
and hence betoken the person who may not be wholly trust-
worthy. Similarly, large or knotted knuckles are the mark
of a thoughtful, calculative mind, while smooth fingers suggest one that is more intuitive. The latter type of person is
guided by his feelings, not controlled by his thoughts.

Such variable characteristics require cautious analysis and
need to be judged along with each other before an accurate
assessment can be made. But there are certain hand features
that have a primal meaning, which is not altered to any great
extent by development, or lack of development, elsewhere
in the hand.

24

If you close your fingers together and then extend them so
that your fingernails are uppermost, you may find that the
end of your index fingers reach to the base of the nail of
the fingers next to them, the middle fingers. If so, they have
a normal or standard length. Should your index fingers fail
to reach the nail base of the middle fingers, they are short;
if they extend further, they are long.

Now the index fingers, known to palmists as the Jupiter
fingers, symbolize the ego or self, and their length represents
the size of one's ego. Hence if your index fingers have a normal length, they reveal that your view of yourself is realis-
tic and balanced, that you do not, in other words, either
undervalue or overvalue yourself or your abilities, and that

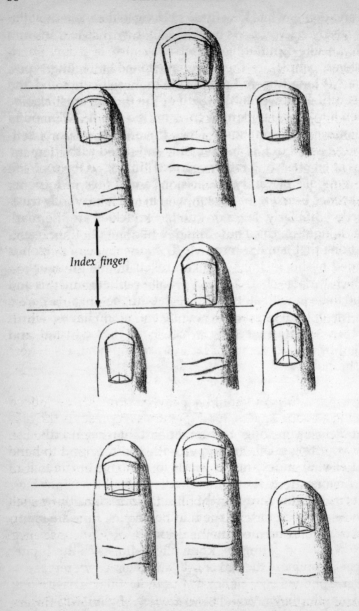

Index finger

Figure 18: The normal, short, and long index fingers

as a consequence you are able to interact with the world in a tolerably harmonious way. This means that you stand a good chance of being happy.

Such is not the case, however, if your index fingers are short or long, for these abnormal lengths symbolize the difficulty you have in seeing yourself as you really are.

If you possess short index fingers they indicate that you undervalue yourself, that you have, in other words, an inferiority complex, whose size is directly related to the fingers' lack of length. And because you will thus go through life thinking, if only at a subconscious level, that you are not worth much, it is very hard for you to feel happy with yourself or with what you do or achieve.

By contrast, if your index fingers are long, they show you have a superiority complex, which means that you think that your ideas, qualities and talents are better or greater than they really are, so causing you to believe mistakenly that you are rather special. Such a distorted self-view similarly makes it difficult for you to relate normally to your fellows, which in turn means that you are likely to feel isolated and unhappy.

Your index fingers should ideally be straight, as indeed should all your fingers, for straightness represents the normal development of the qualities that they symbolize. However, it is quite common for the index fingers to bend towards the middle or Saturn fingers, or conversely to lean away from them.

As the middle fingers symbolize the conscience, any such bending of your index fingers, if present, reveals an abnormal reaction of your ego to the demands of your conscience.

25

Should your index fingers bend towards your middle fingers, and the degree of bending of your right hand index finger is the most important in this respect, it shows that you are particularly sensitive to the demands of your conscience, and that you therefore have a strict set of rules about how to behave and how to run your life. This psychological 'binding' often manifests as a strong need to do things in the way that you think they should be done, as in other words a fixity of purpose, which can be a strength if your desires are possible and worthwhile, but a character weakness if they are not. Such determination may be misinterpreted by others as selfishness, yet it is really imposed on you by the way that you were brought up.

And conversely, if your index fingers bend away from your middle fingers, they reveal that your ego is not bound by the dictates of your conscience, so that you are in essence a free spirit, one unimpeded by guilt or moral doubt. Thus you have little concern for convention or for what others think of you, which means that you will proceed through life seeking out that which is best and most pleasant for yourself. You are thus inclined to be selfish, and people may not trust you completely.

Straight index fingers symbolize an ego which is neither restrictively bound by the conscience nor completely free of its moral influence. Hence if you have straight index fingers, you enjoy liberty without licence and self-expression without guilt. In these respects you have a better chance of finding happiness than if your index fingers bend sideways.

Other facets of character are symbolized by the flexibility of the thumbs, which in themselves represent one's will power and resolve. For this test, all you have to do is turn your palms up towards you, straighten out your fingers, and then open your thumbs as wide as they will go from the side of your hands. You may then find that they open to 90 degrees, so forming a right angle with the side of your hands, or they may not open this far, thus forming an acute angle, or they may open wider than 90 degrees, to an obtuse angle. One thumb may open to a different angle from the other, the right hand thumb angle being larger then the left, or vice versa. These angles of opening of your thumbs are a measure of your self-confidence.

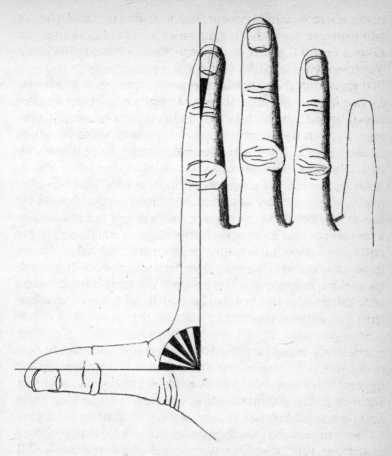

Figure 19: Inward-bending index finger, and thumb opening to 90°

26

If you are unable to open your thumbs to 90 degrees, then you lack confidence in yourself, which is less the smaller the angle of opening. Such self-doubt makes it difficult for you to be happy or to do things that you would like to do, due to the fact that you are pessimistic about your chances of finding success. Indeed, because you may feel that you are not worth very much, this may lead you to believe that you do not deserve much. Such an attitude necessarily casts a shadow over your life.

A greater angle of opening reveals more self-confidence, Hence if your thumbs open to a right angle, they symbolize a confidence that accurately reflects your talents and abilities. You possess, in other words, honest confidence, which enables you to take a pride in your strengths while admitting to your weaknesses. It is an attitude that helps you to be happy with yourself and with your life.

But if your thumbs open to an obtuse angle, they show that while you have plenty of confidence, it is based on an unrealistic evaluation of yourself and your abilities. You are therefore over-confident, perhaps even conceited and arrogant. Your sense of superiority separates you from other people, which negatively affects your relations with them, and may eventually trip you up as you do not have the talent that you believe yourself to have. Happiness could therefore elude you.

The angle of opening of the right thumb is the most important because it symbolizes the amount of confidence that you actually feel, whereas the left thumb opening shows the amount of confidence that you inherited. If your right thumb cannot open as widely as your left thumb, then your upbringing or early experience of the world has prevented you from fully developing your inherited potential. But should the opposite be the case, with your right thumb opening wider than the left, it signifies that you have acquired more self-confidence than you were born with. In both hands, of course, the thumbs should ideally open to 90 degrees.

The placement or setting of your thumbs on the side of your hands represents your degree of caution or openness, a trait which, together with your confidence, largely determines how you interact with the world. High-set thumbs emerge from the hands close to the fingers, while low-set thumbs lie close to the wrist. Thumbs that are medium-set have a more central position.

27

High-set thumbs symbolize caution and thus a lack of openness and warmth. If you have thumbs of this type, they show that you are an inhibited, conservative type, who dislikes

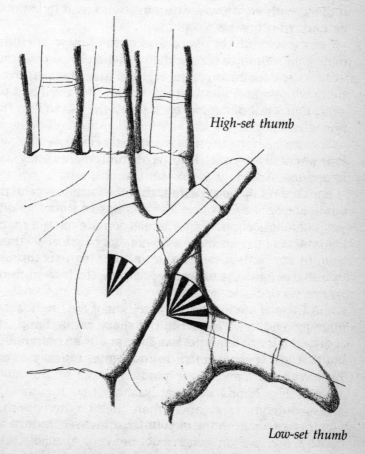

High-set thumb

Low-set thumb

Figure 20: The low-set, and the high-set, thumb

making quick decisions and who resists changing course. Thus you prefer what you know, and you are happiest with the familiar.

Low-set thumbs, by contrast, reveal a far more open attitude to life. Hence if your thumbs are low-set you are comfortable with change, enjoy new ideas, and like meeting different people. In these respects you are friendlier and more outgoing and adventurous than your high-set thumbed opposite. These character traits find an extreme expression in those with very low-set thumbs, who tend to be unstable and irresponsible.

You are basically balanced and centred in your attitude to life if your thumbs are middle-set, whereby you avoid the coolness and inhibition of the high-set thumbed person and the brashness and instability of the low-set thumbed person. Such a middling approach will help you to find happiness and contentment.

The setting of the thumbs is naturally closely linked with their angle of opening. High-set thumbs cannot normally be opened as widely as low-set thumbs, which indicates, as perhaps might be expected, that the former type of person is not only cooler and less responsive than the latter, but is also less confident, whereas confidence is a natural component of the warmer and more outgoing low-set thumb type. In fact in psychological terms, the high-set thumb is a symbol of introversion and repression, the low-set thumb of extroversion and licence.

The angle of opening and the setting of the thumbs must be interpreted with regard to the shape of the hands. Let us take the four Elemental hand shapes as an example. Air and Fire hand people are intrinsically more extroverted than those with Earth and Water hands, yet high-set thumbs on Air and Fire hands necessarily show that the character is less outgoing and open than might otherwise have been expected, in the same way that low-set thumbs will identify the person who may be very unstable. And similarly, high-set thumbs on an Earth and Water hand suggest a tense, blinkered personality, while low-set thumbs reveal more warmth and openness.

As was mentioned earlier, the hands can also tell you which is the dominant hemisphere of your brain. Since the right hemisphere governs the left side of the body, and vice versa, if you are right-handed your left hemisphere is dominant, and if you are left-handed your right hemisphere is dominant.

Researchers D.C. Rife and H. Cromwell used a variety of unimanual operations, such as writing, throwing, sawing, and hammering, to determine handedness. They said that if a person used only his right hand for all these activities, he or she was quite definitely right-handed. But if the left hand was used for one or more of them, then he was to be classified as left-handed. The present author, for example, writes with his left hand but hammers, saws, holds scissors, threads a needle, etc. with his right hand: he is, therefore, left-handed. Ambidextrous people can use either hand with equal facility. Not surprisingly they are rare birds.

28

Left-handed people, particularly those who are predominantly left-handed, not only belong to a minority group— about 10 per cent of the population—but can also suffer from certain problems linked to their hand bias, as well as enjoying a number of advantages. 'If you are left-handed,' says Professor Norman Geschwind of the Harvard Medical Centre, 'you will be prone to certain diseases, but will also be more likely to be artistic, mathematical, and good at judging distances and speeds—as are sportsmen. The benefits will balance the deficits.'

Indeed, if you are left-handed you will be interested to know that you are more likely to have experienced learning difficulties than the average right-hander, and that you are susceptible to epilepsy, immune diseases, and migraine headaches. But take comfort from the fact that recent research carried out at the University of Kansas has shown that you are also more likely to be independent-minded.

Short   Long   Fan-shaped

Figure 21: Fingernail types

Next, take a look at your fingernails. Does the length of that part of them attached to the fingers exceed the width, or are they wider than they are long? And do you perhaps have nails that are fan-shaped? (See Figure 21). The length and shape of your nails are a measure of your irritability and your temper.

29

Short nails are the mark of an inherent irritability and of logical thought processes, and hence of an argumentative and critical disposition. Thus if you have nails of this type you do not suffer fools gladly, and you are easily provoked. Short nails likewise indicate a predisposition for diseases of the heart, which may have already made an appearance if the nails are thin, white in colour, and lacking in their moons.

Long nails symbolize a more easy-going and even-tempered nature. Indeed, if you have long nails, you are likely to also have an intuitive mind and an artistic temperament. Yet your physical constitution may not be strong, as you are prone to lung and chest disorders. If your long nails possess large moons, then you have an over-active thyroid gland.

Fan-shaped nails betoken an anxious disposition, which predisposes their owner to phobias and other psychological disorders. If white flecks are visible beneath the nails—and this applies to nails of whatever length or shape—they will have been caused by a period of heightened stress and anxiety. As it takes each white fleck approximately six months to travel from the base of the nail to its free end, its position in the nail is a guide to how long ago the worrying time was. A fleck lying half-way along the nail, for example, will have been formed about three months earlier.

The skin patterns of the fingertips form the characteristic fingerprints which are so important for the identification and detection of criminals. These unique markings are also believed to symbolize our character and personality, and possibly also our destiny. Indeed, the art of dactylomancy has a long history in Japan, where a considerable amount of study and research into the characterological significance of fingerprints has been done.

There are three basic fingerprint patterns: the arch, which is the simplest, the loop, and the whorl, which is the most complex. Loops may either lean towards the thumb, when they are known as radial loops, or towards the outer edge of the hand, when they are called ulna loops (see Figure 22).

Each pattern type has a number of variations, of which the most important are shown in Figure 23. The tented arch, for instance, is produced by the skin pattern lines flowing over and around an upright central core. Twinned loops, as the name suggests, consist of two loops lying snuggled up to one another the opposite way around. And whorls are either formed by the skin pattern lines arranging themselves in concentric circles (see Figure 22) or by a skin pattern line spiralling in on itself (see Figure 23).

In 1975 Dr Gerald Fox, a psychologist at London's Birkbeck College, fingerprinted 100 volunteers and then gave each of them a test known as the Eysenck Personality Inventory, which measures how introverted or extroverted the subject is and his or her level of stability or neuroticism. This allowed him to see if there is any correlation between these

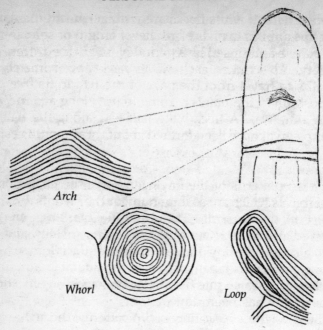

Arch

Whorl

Loop

Figure 22: *The three basic fingerprint patterns*

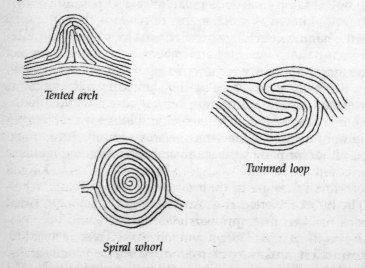

Tented arch

Twinned loop

Spiral whorl

Figure 23: *The tented arch, the twinned loop, and the spiral whorl*

aspects of the personality and the fingerprint types.

Dr Fox did not find any link between the fingerprints of his subjects and their degree of introversion or extroversion, but he did discover that certain types of fingerprints were associated with neuroticism.

30

According to the results of Dr Fox's research, if your hands bear one or more tented arches or twinned loops, or both, which are comparatively rare fingerprint patterns, you have a stable personality. Thus you are, in other words, adaptable, easy-going, optimistic, and hopeful. And should they bear a complete selection of the main fingerprint patterns, that is, if arches, loops, and whorls are present, then you are a very stable type.

But if your fingers lack either tented arches or twinned loops, or if your fingerprint patterns are all of one type, or if indeed you lack the variety of types mentioned above, you have a neurotic or unstable personality. This means that you are anxious, pessimistic, unadaptable, and possibly obsessional.

The Japanese dactylomancer Kojima says that if you possess a mixture of whorls and loops, but no arches, it means that you are honest, kind and truthful, yet because you are impatient but have difficulty in making up your mind, you are also indecisive and unsettled.

Arches are the simplest fingerprint pattern, which is why they are linked with atavistic or elementary character traits, such as selfishness, repression, stubbornness, and a lack of sensitivity. In fact when arches are found in the hand, Kojima claims that they reveal their owner to be ambitious, rebellious, stubborn, and earthy. And interestingly enough, radial loops betoken the same personality dimension.

By contrast, ulnar loops symbolize openness, versatility, cheerfulness, and a love of freedom, which are positive traits, but also lack of perseverance, which is not. It follows that the more ulnar loops you have, the more will your personality be moulded by these characteristics. Yet if you have ulna loops on all your fingers, Kojima says you are gracious and self-controlled, although somewhat depressive, while in your business dealings you can be quite ruthless.

Whorl fingerprint patterns are symbolic of individual character traits such as independence, optimism, and energy, and also manual dexterity and creativity. And again, the more whorls you have, the more marked will these traits be in your personality. This is why Kojima says that when a person has whorls on all his (or her) fingers, he is restless, vacillating, clever, sceptical, enjoys activity, but may be tempted to break the law.

Perhaps more contentious is the notion that our fingerprints can also reveal our fate. Fingerprint reading is not a fortune-telling method that is widely known in the West, but it has a long history, and indeed is still practised in Japan, China, and India. The Chinese formula given below, quoted by H. Cummins and C. Midlo in their book *Finger Prints, Palms and Soles*, shows how one's fortune can be determined by the number of whorls appearing in the hands:

> One whorl, poor; two whorls, rich;
> Three whorls, four whorls, open a pawnshop;
> Five whorls, be a go-between;
> Six whorls, be a thief;
> Seven whorls, meet calamities;
> Eight whorls, eat chaff;
> Nine whorls and one loop, no work to do—
> eat till you are old.

The reader who is interested in learning more about dactylomancy (literally 'divination by the fingers') might like to examine the relevant section of my book *Fortune-Telling by Palmistry*.

The bracelet creases or wrist lines are another interesting and significant 'hand' feature (see Figure 24) which can be interpreted with regard to health, longevity, and fortune.

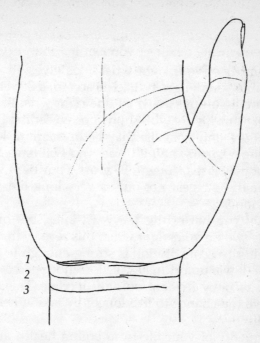

Figure 24: The bracelet creases

There may be one, two, three or occasionally four wrist lines on each wrist. They typically occur on the inside of the wrists, although they sometimes curve around on to the backs.

The bracelet creases should ideally be clearly marked, unbroken, pink in colour, and run straight across the wrist from one side to the other. Less propitious wrist lines are weakly marked, wandering in course, broken, pale in colour, and islanded or chained, or show one or more of these negative features.

Three is the ideal number of wrist lines to have on each wrist, although exceptional people often have four. The lines visible on your left wrist signify your inherited qualities and your potential, while those of your right wrist reveal what you make of these. Hence it is the condition of your right bracelet creases which is the most important.

31

The number of your right wrist lines gives an immediate insight into your longevity. Each is accorded 30 years of time. Therefore if you possess only one right wrist line, it signifies that your life may be short, not exceeding 30 years; if two are present, your life may be of medium length, not exceeding 60 years; and if three, you will have a long life, one that may last as long as 90 years. Four right wrist lines, a rare mark, suggest not only a very long life, but also a healthy one.

Should you have three left wrist lines, but only one or perhaps two on your right wrist, this reveals that although your inherited constitution is strong enough to give you a long life, it will unfortunately be foreshortened by your own bad habits, or by accident, suicide, or crime. This means that you have the chance to live longer by taking better care of yourself.

The quality of your life from both a health and fortune point of view is revealed by the condition of the lines. If they are clearly marked and unbroken, they presage good health and a favourable fate.

Three well-marked bracelet creases are the ideal number to have: these indicate a long, fortunate, healthy, and happy life. But should the right ones be broken or chained, or defective in some other way, then while the life will be long, it will be troubled and difficult. Their owner will not, in other words, be blessed by fortune.

Two well-marked right wrist lines are a sign of a moderately fortunate life. Should you have two such lines, you will achieve certain of your goals and be moderately happy, although you will not rise very high in the world.

One bracelet crease on the right wrist, even if clearly marked, is a sign of difficulty and ill-luck which will naturally be worse if the line is defective.

If you are a woman and your first wrist bracelet curves

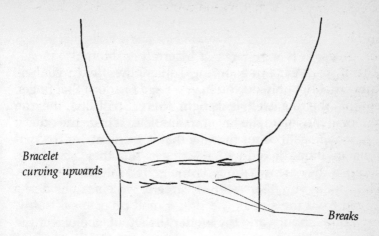

Figure 25: Bracelet crease defects

upwards towards the palm of your hand (see Figure 25), it warns that you are likely to suffer from gynaecological problems and from complications in childbirth.

Breaks in your wrist lines foretell accidents, or illnesses, or sudden upsetting events, the effects of which will last for the length of time indicated by the width of the break. This can be estimated by comparing the width of the break to the width of your wrist, which as we have already discovered symbolizes 30 years. But if the ends of the lines overlap at the break its significance is greatly reduced, which means that the event itself will be less serious or life-threatening.

The wearing of both rings and wrist-watches is common enough, yet their presence goes beyond mere decoration or time-telling. Each can, in fact, reveal much about the psychology of the wearer. The same is also true of tattoos.

Do you wear a ring? If yes, it may be that it is an engagement or wedding ring worn on the third finger of your left hand. Such a ring is normally worn to satisfy convention and may therefore be discounted as a psychological indicator, unless it is very large or bizarrely-fashioned.

Yet if you wear a ring (or rings) on another finger, you will know that not only do you have a need to adorn that finger, but that the ring itself 'feels right' there. So placed, the ring attracts attention to the finger and isolates it from the others, whereby it symbolizes the way that you feel about the personal qualities linked with the finger: that they 'stand out' because they are not properly integrated into your psyche. This causes you distress, the degree of which can be determined from the size of the ring. Small rings speak softly, large ones shout—and the louder the shout, the bigger the problem. The ring also serves as a warning to others, while at the same time asking for their understanding and compassion. With the ring you are silently saying, 'I am a dysfunctioning person, take care.' And lastly, the ring, by giving a subliminal warning of your disturbed state, helps to excuse you from blame should another be hurt by your attitudes or behaviour. You are telling the world, in other words, that you are not wholly responsible for your actions.

A ring or rings worn on your left hand refer to personality disorders which you inherited, whereas right hand rings symbolize those that are acquired.

32

The index fingers symbolize our ego or self, hence if one or other of yours is adorned with a ring it means that you subconsciously feel that your ego demands are excessive, that you are, in other words, proud, selfish and grasping. You may thus be consumed by ambition and want nothing more than to acquire money, power, and fame. Quite often those who wear such rings possess short index fingers, which betoken, as we have already seen, an inferiority complex. This implies that the ambition and the desire for dominance are an attempt by the ego to bolster its low self-esteem.

The middle fingers symbolize our censor or conscience, which you feel to be overly strict and personally limiting if you wear a ring on one or other of them. You thus measure others by your own standards, an attitude that may make you into a carper, a critic and a complainer. Indeed, few things in life will satisfy the expectation that you have of them.

The third fingers symbolize our intuitive powers and our emotions, which you feel are not being properly expressed if you wear a ring on one or both of your own. This may be because you have no suitable outlet for your intuitive/ emotional instincts, or because you are emotionally repressed. A third finger ring may also signify that your intuitive insights are being ignored by your brain's logical left hemisphere. Your lack of expression in these respects adversely affects your happiness.

The fourth or little fingers relate to sex and to our intimate relationships, whose demands are troubling if you wear a ring on either, or both, of yours. Sexual anxieties may be caused by guilt about sex, or they may stem from the nature of our sexual needs, which may be in conflict with the dictates of conventional morality. Either way, they make it difficult for the afflicted to enjoy harmonious close relationships.

When we buy a watch we choose one that is not only aesthetically pleasing but which also reflects our personality, or at least the image that we would like to project. And in these respects, the watch strap is as significant as the watch itself. The image-conscious person often possesses two or more different types of watch, whose design is chosen to suit the occasion. For example, a man might prefer to wear a heavy, solid-looking watch at work to express his authority, but opt for one that is smarter and less forbidding when he goes to a party, when he hopes to appear charming and interesting to the opposite sex. But while a watch needs interpreting with care, it always has something useful to say about its owner.

33

If you wear one of the watch types listed below, it reveals the following facts about you:

1 **a pocket watch**: you are conventional, reflective, nostalgic, interested in social issues, yet rather anxious. You only feel comfortable when you have everything under control.

2 **a large-dialled watch with a heavy expanding strap**: you are immature, energetic, excitable, boastful, lecherous, and lacking in refinement.

3 **a slimline watch with a leather strap**: you are smooth, well-mannered, responsible, serious-minded, earnest, conservative, and tasteful.

4 **a digital display watch**: you are shallow, over-eager, talkative, light-hearted, emotionally-troubled, and lacking in self-esteem.

5 **a watch with several dials**: you are a dreamer, impractical, changeable, lacking in concentration, unsociable, and generally pessimistic.

6 **a small watch with a tiny dial**: you are either a normal woman, or if you are a man you are insecure, shallow, talkative, fussy, and possibly effeminate.

7 **a Mickey Mouse or other cartoon character watch**: you are either childish and emotionally undeveloped, or you are a sour, miserable person trying to pretend that you are a bundle of fun.

The commonest form of body contact we have with strangers is handshaking, a practice that probably originated among Roman soldiers, who clasped one another's sword-hands as a sign of friendship. Handshaking is still used to signify a conflict resolved, although it is normally employed as a means of introduction, greeting, and congratulation. We all know that different people's hands have both a different feel and a different way of clasping our own, some conveying an impression of vigour and confidence, while others signal weakness and uncertainty. In fact it has been said that while a smile or the manner of another can deceive, the handshake can never lie. Some of the more unpleasant handshake styles, and what they say about those who employ them, are described below.

34

1   **The Dead Fish**: the proffered hand feels like a cold, wet, and boneless piece of fish. This is perhaps the most repellant handshake to encounter, although its owner is not usually quite as bad. He (or she) is, however, emotionally cold, passionless, and lacking in life and vitality, which is why he is difficult to interest or arouse. He won't hear what you say to him, so don't bother trying to communicate.

2   **The Pumper**: this person shakes your hand enthusiastically and can't seem to stop, almost as if he fears that you may run off if he did. Shy people lacking in confidence often have this handshaking style, which they use to cover up their social inadequacy. Hence they are more to be pitied than censured. Yet over-eager salesmen sometimes use this handshake, as do those who are inherently foolish.

3   **The Shower**: the hand is very moist and clammy, yet is not necessarily lacking in life or substance. This handshake belongs to the person who is chronically nervous and whose belief in himself is not great. Interestingly, J. Edgar Hoover, a former director of the CIA, believed that wet palms signified a bad character, and would not hire those who had them.

4   **The Crusher**: this is the hand that grips yours with such force that your bones crack. It is favoured by the man who is secretly uncertain of his masculinity, but who wishes to convey a macho impression with his muscular strength. Many homosexuals use this style of handshake.

5   **The Quick Touch**: the hand fails to make proper contact with yours and withdraws itself as soon as it has

touched you. This person is misanthropic and thus dislikes body contact. Hence don't expect to make a friend of him or her. It is also used by those who wish to convey to you that they think you are of little consequence. Yet such an attitude really shows that they don't think much of themselves.

Chapter Four
BODY MOVEMENTS

In some fair body thus th' informing soul
With spirit feeds, with vigour fills the whole,
Each motion guides, and ev'ry nerve sustains;
Itself unseen, but in th' effects, remains.

Our bodies speak, not only by their size and shape, but by the way in which we hold and move them. We all know that sagging shoulders and a drooping head betoken despondency, while the happy and positive person holds these parts erect. Our qualities of character, along with our mood, are also mirrored in our stance and carriage, which means that if we can interpret the latter, we will intimately know the former. And such an ability can not only give knowledge of others, but also of oneself.

Take the way that you walk, for example, which has been more recently investigated and analysed by Sara E. Snodgrass, a psychologist at Skidmore College, Saratoga Springs, New York, who believes that our walking style reveals the type of person that we are. In this regard Dr Snodgrass has some notable antecedents, the most eminent of whom was Aristotle, who noted: 'He or she that goes slowly, making great steps as they go, are generally persons of bad memory, and dull of apprehension, given to loitering, and not apt to believe what is told them. He who goes apace, and makes short steps, is most successful in all his undertakings, swift in his imagination, and humble in the disposition of his affairs. He who makes wide and uneven steps, and side-long withal, is one of a greedy sordid nature, subtle, malicious, and willing to do evil.'

35

Dr Snodgrass says that, if you walk with a bounce, taking long strides and swinging your arms, it signifies that you are self-assured, friendly, happy, and ambitious, whereas if you take short strides and drag your feet, or if your style of walking is uneven and choppy, you lack these outgoing characteristics. She found that people who are frustrated and unhappy tend to drag their feet, and that those who are impulsive 'duck walk', that is, apply the whole of their foot surface to the ground at each step, instead of the heel first. The dominant person, by contrast, walks with an overkick and dips down somewhat with each stride.

If you are a woman, Dr Snodgrass says that your arm-swing is particularly important. If you swing out your arms when walking, you are likely to be a high-achiever and are less likely to be depressed, or angry, or frustrated and con-fused, than a woman who hardly swings her arms at all.

The most useful outcome of this research is the discovery that by adopting a 'positive' style of walking, by holding one-self erect and stepping out, one can promote positive inner feelings, in the same way that by putting on a happy face, one can improve one's mood. For our moods are not, as we all too often assume, created solely by outside influences, but are really the result of how we allow ourselves to react to them. And by making an effort to cheer ourselves up, we make ourselves more attractive to others, whose favour-able response will further lift our mood. There is, after all, much truth in the saying, 'Laugh, and the world laughs with you; cry, and you cry alone.'

Walking has recently come back into fashion as a healthy form of exercise, and indeed the benefits of a brisk walk are great when you consider both its mental and physical advantages. Yet today's man or woman is still more likely to be found in a gymnasium or body shop, or jogging, than taking a stroll. And interestingly, a recent study of the exercise habits of 19,000 men and women aged between 18 and 64, carried out by Christine Brooks at the University of Michigan at Ann Arbor, has shown that those with a particular type of personality tend to work out the most.

36

If you are the sort of person who works out regularly, at least once a week, then you are likely to be what Dr Brooks calls 'inner-directed'—that is, you are self-motivating, set your own goals, and feel that you are very much in control of your life. However, should you take little or no exercise, then you are probably 'outer-directed', which means that you tend to accept things as they are, be guided by the opinion and expectations of others, and think that you have little control over what happens to you in life.

But there is regular exercise and compulsive regular exercise, and the compulsive jogger or weight-lifter who feels driven to exercise no matter what, is likely to be anything but well-adjusted and 'inner-directed'. In fact he or she is probably an obsessive neurotic, a person torn by doubt and self-loathing, who tries to compensate for such distressing inner feelings by keeping super-fit. It is no accident that many dedicated joggers are middle-aged men who are either divorced or experiencing marital problems, who have reached the peak of their middle-management careers, and who feel lonely, misunderstood, resentful, and unattractive. Thus it comes as no surprise to learn, according to a study done by the Gewis Institute in Hamburg, Germany, that 40 per cent of male joggers fantasize about sex or that 10 per cent dwell on the difficulties they are having at home, whereas female joggers tend to concentrate on such things as clothes and cooking, with only 5 per cent thinking about sex or partnership problems.

The way that you walk and carry yourself not only reflects your inner feelings. It may also determine if you are likely to become a mugging victim. Muggers are opportunistic thieves, who strike when they come across someone they believe won't give them much, or any, trouble. As the only clues they have to go on come from the potential victim's appearance, those showing signs of vulnerability get chosen in preference to individuals with a positive, confident image.

Professor Pelly Grayson, of Hofstra University, New York, showed over 100 short films taken of people walking along a street to convicted muggers at Rahway State Penitentiary, New York, and asked them to pick out the 'easy victims'. The muggers selected 20 who fell, they said, into that category, and Professor Grayson noted that there were five movement characteristics common to all of them. It follows that if you display these, you stand a greater chance of getting mugged than someone who does not.

37

The potential mugging victim's movement characteristics are:

1 The 'duck walk' stride, whereby the whole of the foot undersurface is both lifted from, and placed back on, the ground, instead of the heel being applied to, and the toes lifting from, it.
2 The stride is exaggerated, being either too long or too short.
3 The right arm is swung forward with the right leg and the left arm with the left leg, instead of alternately.
4 The upper part of the body moves at cross-purposes to the lower half, the right shoulder moving in conjunction with the left hip and the left shoulder similarly accompanying the right hip.

5   The arm and leg movements appear to 'come from outside the body instead of from within'.

Taking a walk may eventually bring you into contact with someone you know, or at least someone to whom you stop and talk, and how you stand and talk can reveal things about you both. Shy people, for example, do not like getting too close to others, and if they can pluck up the courage to stop the other person from entering their personal space, they will stand on average eight inches farther away from him than will someone who is bolder, say psychologists Bernardo Carducci and Art Webber.

38

Carducci's and Webber's research, which they carried out with Californian university students, showed that the shy stand about 33 inches away from a person of their own sex, while those rated less shy move in to an average distance of 25 inches.

The shy stand even farther away from someone of the opposite sex—at an average distance of 36.3 inches—while the less shy edge marginally closer, to an average distance of 24.4 inches.

These observations give you a rough and ready way of evaluating your own shyness. If you feel most comfortable standing about three feet from another person, then this marks you out as shy, whereas if two feet or thereabouts is right for you, such closeness suggests that you are pretty confident. Standing distances also give you the opportunity of judging how shy others are by watching how close they are prepared to get to one another.

If you are shy, you can take some comfort from the fact that you are not alone. Indeed, a recent study conducted by British psychologist Peter Harris found that 41 per cent of the interviewees considered themselves to be shy. And shyness can prevent its sufferers from enjoying their lives and making the most of their opportunities. 'Shyness can be as serious as clinical depression,' says Harris, 'and can even shift into agoraphobia at its most serious stage. And yet it's still treated as a childish disease and not really taken seriously.' But while the very shy may require professional help in coping with their condition, all shy people need sympathy, support, and encouragement, from their families and friends.

Once you have noted the distance apart that you and your conversational partner decide to stand, take special note of what is said to you, because according to Dr Walter Weintraub, a psychiatrist at the University of Maryland, 'verbal behaviour is representative of general behaviour'. Indeed, Dr Weintraub has discovered that what a man or woman says in 10 minutes is sufficient to reveal their personality type. Special attention must be given to 14 speech characteristics, which include (1) the talking speed (2) the number of references to 'I' and 'me', and (3) the use of qualifiers like 'I think' and 'kind of' that add uncertainty to what is said. The frequency of 'retractor' words, such as 'but', 'although', 'nevertheless', and 'however', which often cancel or contradict what has been said beforehand, is also very important.

39

If your conversational partner uses a lot of retractive words or phrases, and if he often refers to himself and his feelings, then he is probably an impulsive type, who makes hasty judgements and tends to act before he thinks. Impulsive people create problems for themselves by their actions, as they tend to speak out of turn or at the wrong moment, buy items that they don't need or can't afford, and make decisions which may ultimately be to their disadvantage.

But if he (or she), by contrast, talks mainly about himself, making great use of the personal pronouns 'I' and 'me', and employing many negative words, 'feeling' phrases, and long reflective silences, then his conversation reveals that he has depressive tendencies and is therefore far from happy with life.

And if your acquaintance or friend uses a lot of explanatory expressions, which typically begin with 'as', 'because', and 'since', he is showing signs of paranoia. 'These stem', observes Dr Weintraub, 'from the paranoid's need to rationalize far-fetched beliefs.

Yet what is said by someone may be less important to the listener than the quality of his voice, for nonsense spoken in mellifluous tones is often more persuasive than a harsh, unpleasant voice talking sense. Indeed, we are more often judged by our voices than by what we say, which is perhaps why Aristotle claimed that a person's character can be known by his (or her) way of talking. He said that a voice which is full yet mild, and pleasant to the ear, 'shows the person to be of a quiet and peaceful disposition (which is a great virtue, and rare to be found in a woman) and also very thrifty and secret, not prone to anger, but of a yielding temper.' Aristotle described less well modulated voices as being indicative of the character traits listed below.

40

1 A loud, full voice: betokens confidence, cheerfulness, pride, and wilfulness.
2 A loud, shrill, yet not unpleasant voice: reveals thrift, cleverness, wisdom, and honesty, but also vanity, credulity, and capriciousness.
3 A loud, shrill, and unpleasant voice: betrays ambition, selfishness, anger, and quarrelsomeness, yet also energy and courage.
4 A faint, weak voice: is linked with a clever and imaginative mind, but also with physical weakness, poor appetite, and timidity.
5 A weak, trembling voice: betokens suspicion, envy, weakness, fear, and slow wits.
6 A rough, hoarse voice: reveals a slow-moving, dull, and unimaginative person.

7 A voice rising to a higher note: a sign of self-confidence and boldness, but also of anger and violence.

A volume of the *Philosophical Transactions and Collections* published in 1700 contains an interesting addendum to Aristotle. Titled 'A conjecture at dispositions from the modulation of the voice', its author therein observed:

Sitting in some company, and having been but a little before musical, I chanced to take notice, that in ordinary discourse *words* were spoken in perfect *notes*; and that some of the company used *eighths*, some *fifths*; some *thirds*; and that his discourse which was most pleasing, his *words*, as to their tone, consisted most of *concords*, and were of *discords* of such as made up harmony. The same person was the most affable, pleasant, and best natured in the company. This suggests a reason why many discourses which one *hears* with much pleasure, when they come to be *read* scarcely seem the same things.

From this difference of Music in SPEECH, we may conjecture that of TEMPERS. We know, the Doric mood sounds gravity and sobriety; the Lydian, buxomness and freedom, the Aeolic, sweet stillness and quiet composure; the Phrygian, jollity and youthful levity; the Ionic is a stiller of storms and disturbances rising from passion. And why may we not reasonably suppose, that those whose speech naturally runs into the notes peculiar to any of these moods, are likewise in nature hereunto congenerous? *C Fa ut* may show me to be of an ordinary capacity, though good disposition. *G sol re ut*, to be peevish and effeminate. *Flats*, a manly or melancholic sadness. He who hath a voice which will in some measure agree with all *clefs*, to be of good parts, and fit for a variety of employments, yet somewhat of an inconstant nature. Likewise from the TIMES: so *semi-briefs*, may speak a temper dull and phlegmatic; *minims*, grave and serious; *crotchets*, a prompt wit; *quavers*, a vehemency of passion, and scolds use them. *Semi-brief rest*, may denote one either stupid or fuller of thoughts than he can utter them; *minim-rest*, one that deliberates; *crotchet-rest*, one in a passion.

Now consider, when you are at home or at work, in a space that you regard as your own, do you keep it nice and tidy? Or are your habits more slovenly? Your answer is important, because your attitude towards your surroundings also reflects your personality, and being excessively tidy or extremely sloppy can be symptomatic of inner difficulties.

41

If you are the type of person who does not feel at ease, or who cannot function, unless your home or office desk is spotlessly tidy, such assiduity is symptomatic of psychic disorder, of a feeling that you are out of control, for which you compensate by imposing your control on your surroundings. Speaking of the excessively tidy woman, clinical psychologist Richard Samuels says, 'She may have a domineering mother who didn't give her room to grow. As a result, she focused on her ability to manipulate objects in her own room. In adulthood she claims her home as the one realm she can control. Meanwhile, the rest of her life is often a shambles.'

At work, a compulsive need to keep one's desk tidy reveals similar tendencies. This explains why the person who is obsessive about keeping his desk straight is frequently unable to perform his job well.

But the psychological state of the sloppy and untidy person is equally troubled. For while messiness is popularly associated with laziness, it really signifies mental disharmony in the form of anxiety or depression, or it may be symptomatic of a disordered mind.

If you are a chronically untidy person, take a look around your home to see where the disorder is concentrated. Chaos that is limited to, or worse in, your bedroom, may show that you're in sexual conflict with your partner; if in the living room, that you have problems in socializing with other people; and if in the kitchen, that you are failing to cope with the responsibility of nurturing your family. And such mess, if it is imposed upon others, suggests that you harbour resentments against them.

When you are working at your hopefully not too tidy desk, or attending a meeting, or listening to a lecture, do you sometimes doodle? If yes, keep the next ones that you draw, as they are important clues to the inner you. For example, should you doodle while listening to your boss drone endlessly on about something that doesn't interest you, it may well express the boredom that you are feeling, or the wish that he would either shut up or get to the point, which you are not able to put into words. Yet if you produce essentially the same doodles in a variety of situations, they signify deep-seated feelings that for one reason or another you cannot reveal.

However, it is important to understand what a doodle is. A doodle is only produced when your conscious mind is occupied elsewhere. If you are fully aware of what you are doing, the result is a drawing, not a doodle.

42

Your doodles are unique to yourself, which is what we would expect if they mirror your feelings or your personality, yet because there are a number of commonly occurring motifs portrayed in doodles, they can be interpreted as reflecting similar attitudes and emotions.

One of the simplest types of doodle is the filling in of printed letters, such as those of a newspaper, and if you do this, it shows you to be a tidy, orderly person, who can be relied upon to get on with the job in hand, although you lack initiative and creativity, These personality traits are more strongly developed if you surround several letters with a line and then shade in the contents. Such a doodle reveals that you are very controlled, possibly even obsessive. Should you add to or extend printed letters, then your imagination is greater, although if the extensions take the form of enclosing circles or squares, you pigeon-hole ideas and people, which suggests that you are orderly and have a need to control, where possible, your surroundings.

When a single capital letter forms the basis of your doodle, it is likely to be the initial of somebody's name who is emotionally important to you. If you embellish the letter with graceful designs, they show you that you idealize the person concerned. However, should the letter be one of your own initials, it reveals that you are vain and self-absorbed.

Doodles that have a lot of shading, especially if it is dark and heavily-marked, betoken a dour and pessimistic person, who may be depressed. Contrarily, when the doodle has equal amounts of light and shade, it signifies manic-depressive tendencies, the personality alternating between optimism and despondency. Regular chessboard patterns of light and shade show that the doodler has come to terms with these tendencies, that he has structured them into his psyche, and that he feels they are largely under his control.

If you cover your doodles with cross-hatched lines, particularly if they are sharply and heavily drawn, you have conflicting emotions and obsessive thoughts. But if you draw parallel lines that resemble prison bars across your doodle, it indicates that you have closed in or shut off the feelings symbolized by the doodle. In this sense they are representative of anxiety. Similarly, if you hide your doodle with shading, such concealment means that you need to conceal certain strong feelings or desires, which distress you.

Free-form doodles are symbolic of greater independence and creativity than are those based on printed letters and symbols. They may take the form of geometrical shapes, which perhaps abut or interlock, or they may be representations of familiar objects and scenes, like mountains, valleys, trees, pylons, telegraph poles, roads, rivers, houses, animals, modes of transport, etc. In fact the variety of doodled images is enormous. 'They are very similar to dreams in this regard,' says Dr Albert I. Rabin, Professor of Clinical Psychology at Michigan State University.

In general, circles and rounded shapes symbolize tolerance, sensitivity and passivity, and a more co-operative way of interacting with others, which are all feminine qualities. Squares and rectangles, by contrast, signify a blunter, more masculine approach to life, with an emphasis on logical thought and independent action. Triangular or diamond-shaped doodles betoken a sharpness of manner, bad temper, and aggression. Herringbone patterns are symbolic of impatience and a desire to make progress. Indeed, any repetitively doodled figure is representative of a need for order, and thus a herringbone pattern can symbolize a desire to achieve order by fulfilling one's ambitions or reaching one's goals.

If you doodle concentric circles while listening to a discussion, you are probably thinking that those concerned are going round in circles, to no great effect. But should you place a dot at the centre, or if you have a doodled a target with a similar central point, it indicates that, having heard all sides of the argument, you have come to your own conclusion. And your mind is well and truly made up if you depict a dart or arrow embedded in the target's centre.

You have a wide-ranging and flexible mind if you depict three-dimensional figures, like bricks or pyramids, in your doodles, although you probably have trouble in reaching conclusions and making decisions. But if your doodled figures are many edged or spiky, and have few curved lines, they reveal that you are aggressive and are poorly adjusted in a social sense.

The evaluation of doodled objects and scenes must take into account their overall shape, the amount of shading, if any, the degree of activity portrayed, the ambience of the total picture, etc., while at the same time being aware, where another person is concerned, that you have to, as Dr Rabin says, 'know about the individual and his past in order to fully interpret the doodle.' However, doodles of rounded shapes like ponds, wheels, the sun, and so on, have a calmer and more tolerant and optimistic meaning than those which depict objects that are jagged or pointed, or which are representative of knives, guns and other weapons, these being symbolic of contention and aggression. A house or other building is usually indicative of a sense of security, but if it is shown as being on fire, or in the process of falling down, or is threatened by some other disaster, then the doodler clearly feels that his own security is under threat.

Doodles of open vistas, with perhaps birds flying overhead and a bright sun in the sky, betoken broad views, imagination, hope, and a general *joie de vivre*, although the elevated ideas, symbolized by the birds, may not be very practicable. Conversely, scenes depicting restraining walls and fences, or those of interiors, indicate a lack of freedom, of being hemmed in and held down, which in turn suggest frustration and impotence. If such barriers are doodled by a person attending a meeting, for example, they may signify that he has a point to make but knows that he cannot do so, perhaps because it would be to his ultimate disadvantage.

Dr Rabin claims that if you doodle people who have long necks, it shows that you have a dependent nature, whereas if you doodle boats you have a need for maternal affection. The doodling of dogs, cats, horses and other familiar domesticated animals reveals that you are a normal, well-integrated person, while if you doodle large animals like elephants, or dangerous carnivores like lions and tigers, you probably feel inadequate. In a similar way, you are probably suffering from some type of phobia if you often doodle spiders, earwigs, bats, rats, and other disagreeable creatures.

Lastly, are you unfortunate enough to suffer from a pain that your doctor is unable to cure? If so, it may be caused, not by some physical disorder, but by a negative emotion that you can neither show nor get rid of. Indeed, the pain itself, according to Dr Wouter Oosterhuis, who carried out a survey of 500 pain-racked men and women, is a symptom of the distressing emotion.

43

Dr Oosterhuis claims that if you have a mysterious pain in your neck, it is probably caused by unresolved aggressive feelings, which make you, in more ways than one, a 'pain in the neck'.

Likewise, should your pain be centred in your stomach, it is likely to be caused by fear. You may, for example, be frightened of the future, of illness, of old age, or, if you are a woman, of your husband. Hence your griping.

And if you suffer from a pain in your lower back, just above the buttocks, then you may be suffering from either sorrow or despair. If you allow this to affect your relationship with others adversely, it is hardly surprising that they find you a 'pain in the arse'.

Dr Oosterhuis says that you need help in solving the problem causing your negative emotion, as well as psychological support, which should lead to the curing of your body pain.

Chapter Five

SLEEP AND DREAMING

When at the close of each sad, sorrowing day,
Fancy restores what vengeance snatch'd away,
Then conscience sleeps, and leaving nature free,
All my loose soul unbounded springs to thee.

We sleep on average for eight hours out of every 24, which adds up to an astonishing one third of our lives spent wrapped, as the poets would put it, in the arms of Somnus. This alone suggests that sleep is vital to our health and well-being, and indeed our ability to function effectively is quickly impaired if we are deprived of sleep. Long periods of sleep loss result in hallucinations and mental imbalance.

Hence it is perhaps not surprising that the way in which we sleep, whether or not we remember our dreams, the type of dreams that we have, and the condition of our beds, can reveal much about us. This is why we must examine Somnus's realm with care, for your trysts with the god of sleep are not simply losses of consciousness, but are an expression of your true self.

'You can read a person by his bed,' opines Dr Arvalea Nelson, a staff psychologist at the Berkeley Therapy Institute in California, which, while an overstatement of fact, does contain sufficient truth to make the bed the best place to start.

44

Research has shown that if you don't make your bed and if you fail to change the bed linen regularly, then you probably don't care too much about yourself either, which means you have a poor self-image. Your self-image is far more positive if you make your bed every morning and keep it tidy, and if you also prefer coloured sheets and pillow cases, then you are blessed with an artistic nature. Matching sheets and pillow cases are indicative of a sensible, conservative attitude to life, while mixed pattern bed linen reveals a more independent mind and outlook. Tatty and frayed bed linen is suggestive of both a sloppy attitude to life and a feeling that the best has happened to you and that the future has little to offer. A nesting urge, which includes not only the desire to start a family but also the need to centre your life in the home, is revealed if you store personal possessions, especially those that are treasured, under the bed.

San José sex therapist Mary Buxton has noted that when things are going well in a couple's relationship the 'bed is the centre of excitement'. In fact the positions adopted by a sleeping couple give an insight into how they are getting on. A happy couple sleep close to one another, each taking pleasure and comfort in the proximity of the other. Troubled couples, by contrast, make a space between themselves, each sleeping close to the outer edge of the bed. As the relationship deteriorates, their sleep schedules become disrupted, with one partner staying up later than the other so that intimacy is avoided. Later, they may take to separate bedrooms, a development that may betoken the imminent collapse of their union.

But aside from body spacing between couples, the predominant position adopted by each of us during sleep can provide important clues to our personality and status, one Harley Street psychiatrist even claiming that 'our posture during sleep shows how we react to life's problems'. And while we all toss and turn to varying degrees during sleep, the preferred sleep position is usually the one that we find ourselves in when we wake up in the morning.

There are four principal sleeping postures, although each has a number of variations. The former are described below.

45

1 **The Royal Position:** this is when you sleep on your back with your arms held somewhat apart from your body and your ankles separated. It shows that you have a strong, secure personality and plenty of self-confidence. You believe that anything is possible for you, and you are generous and accepting. Your attitude gives you a sense of command.

2 **The Prone Position:** this is the reverse of the above position—you sleep on your stomach, with your arms extended over your head and your legs stretched out, yet somewhat apart. This position reveals that you are a careful and cautious person, and that you need to feel in control of your life. Indeed, you dislike surprises and uncertainty, and you do your best to avoid them. Yet you are basically happy and well-integrated.

3 **The Full-Foetal Position:** so called because it resembles the curled-up posture of a baby in the womb. You sleep on your side with your knees drawn far up and your arms clasping your body. All anxious people curl up when they sleep, and this position shows that you lack confidence in yourself and have a deep need to be loved and protected. In fact you may find it difficult to develop a completely independent lifestyle for yourself. You function best in a relationship that gives you the same support that you had from your parents.

4 **The Semi-Foetal Position:** this posture is similar to the above, except that the knees are not drawn up so high and the arms do not clasp the body. It is the

commonest sleep position, and it shows that you are quite happy with yourself and feel fairly secure. You can accept challenges, and you deal with the unexpected without experiencing too much stress. But if you also cuddle your pillow, you need affection, while if you dangle one arm over the side of the bed, it shows that there is something you feel guilty about.

Sleep allows us to dream, a vital brain activity and one that is probably more important to us than the physical rest that sleep provides. We know that people who have been deprived of sleep spend an increased amount of time dreaming when they next sleep, which suggests that they have a dream 'debt' to make up.

Sleep research has shown that we all dream an average of three to five times a night, although not everybody recalls dreaming once, never mind remembering the content of their dreams. This fact divides humanity into two groups, the dream rememberers and the dream forgetters, and psychologist Liam Hudson of Edinburgh University says that the two types have quite different personalities.

46

According to Dr Hudson, if you usually remember one or more of your dreams, it shows that you have an adaptable, flexible mind, a good imagination, and that you are open and tolerant in your relationships with others. In this respect he classifies you as a 'diverger'. You may score rather poorly in ordinary IQ tests, but do well in those that test your creativity or your imagination. As a student, you prefer art and the humanities to mathematics and science.

If you belong to the dream forgetter group, you have a more logical and analytical mind, are less open to new and different ideas, and are rather authoritarian in manner. You score better in ordinary IQ tests than in those that focus on imagination and creativity. And you prefer science and mathematics to the arts and the humanities. You tend to think that you are right more often than the person who remembers his dreams. Dr Hudson classifies you on this basis as a 'converger'.

If you have trouble in remembering your dreams, you may find it helpful to sleep with a pad and a pencil at your bedside, and when you wake to record immediately any dream recollections that you have. By doing this regularly you should find that your dream memory gradually improves, or that you will at least get an idea of what you're dreaming about. Keeping a dream diary is also helpful to those who can recall their dreams, for while you may be able to remember a dream on waking, you are sure to forget the less spectacular ones as time passes. The recording of your dreams, moreover, both gives you the opportunity to note the changes that take place in them over a period of time and to examine them more closely.

In ancient times dreams were considered to be messages from the gods, and the dreamer, particularly if he was a person of importance, would relate any exceptional dream that he had to a diviner to have it interpreted. Nowadays we believe that dreams are messages from our unconscious mind, and for their interpretation we turn, when necessary, to a psychiatrist. Yet dreams, while they are often hard to understand, almost invariably relate to things in our lives that are troubling us. And fortunately certain dream motifs are so common that they clearly have a universal meaning, which is why the meaning of the ten commonest dreams are considered below.

47

1   The dream of missing a train (or a bus or a boat, etc.) may symbolize some opportunity, such as a promotion, that has passed you by, or it may mean that you feel that life is passing you by. Alternatively, missing a train can indicate that you feel you have failed to grow up. The overall message of the dream is that

you are being left behind and are not progressing.

2   If you dream of swimming in a river against the current, it means that certain problems or difficulties in life are hindering you from moving forwards. In one sense the dream is less negative than that of missing a train, yet it also points up the fear you have of being swept away or overcome.

3   The dream in which you find yourself falling reveals a fear of failure and suggests that you have anxieties about your position in life. You may, for example, have worries about the stability of your marriage or business, or fear that certain of your actions or traits of character will lead to your undoing.

4   To dream of flying may be one way of compensating for your feelings of inferiority, whereby you rise above all those things in life that make you feel second-rate or insignificant. But flying dreams may also symbolize the maturation of the personality, the ego being at last set free to fly like a bird.

5   If you dream of climbing it may mean that you feel that you are achieving your goals, or it may be a wish fulfilment, whereby you do in your dreams—i.e. rise in the world—what you are unable to do in waking life. For a boy, a climbing dream may symbolize his developing sexuality.

6   Developing female sexuality is often symbolized by the dreamer finding herself being chased, often by a faceless, unidentified man. By representing herself as being pursued, the dreamer dramatizes her desire to lose her virginity (there is a pun on the words 'chased' and 'chaste'). Similarly, being 'rooted to the spot' in a dream reveals the dreamer's fear (symbolized by her immobility) of what might happen if she gratifies her sexual urges.

7   Many women often dream of being naked in a public place. Such dreams are common among women because they are still obliged to take a secondary role in life in favour of their husbands and children.

Hence the dream shows that they wish to 'expose' their true selves and to stop hiding behind the facade that they have erected. Naked dreams are also a wish fulfilment for shy persons of both sexes, who are inhibited from behaving in the way that they would like to.

8 The dream in which you are looking for a room can have several meanings. It may show, for example, that you desire independence, or it may reveal that you are searching for a partner in life, the room symbolizing the home that such a union would bring you. In Freudian psychology a room is a symbol of the womb, thus to dream of looking for a room can mean a desire to return to the security of childhood or even to the womb itself. If the room cannot be found it shows that you feel you have lost your way in life.

9 The dream of descending into a cellar, cave or similar dark place can be frightening. In Freudian terms, a cellar or cave, like a room, represents the womb, and such a dream can symbolize a desire to return to its warmth and protection—and anonymity. However, a cellar or other dark place can also represent the unconscious, and hence to dream of entering it represents your need to confront the troubling psychic elements that reside in your own unconscious. We have long understood that confrontation with the contents of the unconscious is necessary to achieve full psychic integration, as the universal myth of the hero descending into the nether regions and emerging triumphant indicates.

10 To dream that someone has died or that you have committed a murder is the fulfilment of a wish that the person concerned was actually dead. Should you dream of killing a person whom you profess to love, your true feelings for them are thereby revealed. When punishment follows the dream murder, it symbolizes the guilt your hatred has produced.

Chapter Six

PERSONAL QUIRKS

That each from other differs, first confess;
Next, that he varies from himself no less:
Add Nature's, Custom's, Reason's, Passion's strife,
And all Opinion's colours cast on life.

Like most people, you presumably have your own way of doing things and your own likes and dislikes, which you perhaps regard as peculiar to yourself. They are not, of course, but they are expressive of your personality, and it is the purpose of this chapter to examine some of the more common personal quirks, so as to give you further insights into yourself and to help you understand what those of your relatives, friends and workmates say about them.

The first quirk that we will consider, smoking, is a pleasure to those who indulge in it, but a quite disgusting habit to those who don't. In Great Britain, for example, despite all the warnings about the health damage that smoking can cause, which includes the birth of undersized babies, lung cancer, and heart disease, some 17 million citizens still continue with the habit. Anti-smokers would perhaps say that this proves there's no accounting for human stupidity, but in fact it may simply be an expression of a particular type of personality, if we are to believe the results of a survey on smokers and non-smokers that was conducted by Frederick J. Evans, the director of research at the Carrier Foundation in Belle Mead, New Jersey.

Figure 26: James Dean, one of many film stars to smoke tobacco

48

Evans and his team interviewed 1,400 adult smokers and non-smokers, all of whom were given a standard personality test, and it was discovered that the smokers were more worried and anxious, and more likely to be hypochondriacal, which are neurotic traits, and similarly more selfish, hostile and emotionally cold, which are psychotic traits, than people who have never smoked or who once smoked at least ten cigarettes a day but who stopped smoking at least two years previously.

'We found not just a smoker's personality,' commented Evans, 'but a smoke addict's personality. What we actually found is that high scorers on neuroticism smoked to relieve tension, while those high in extroversion smoked in social situations.'

This suggests that if you are a smoker but would like to quit, you stand a better chance of doing so if you can reduce your anxiety, by either learning to relax or by dealing with the cause of your worry, or both.

According to the perfume manufacturers Haarman and Reimer, our personality and our mood type affect our reactions to perfume, and thus decide the scents that we buy. This means that your perfume preferences can serve as a guide to the sort of person that you are.

But first we must examine the terms *extrovert* and *introvert*, which figure prominently in the analysis. Each was used by the Swiss psychiatrist Carl Jung (1875—1961) to identify respectively one of the two primary personality types into which he believed the human race is divided. The extrovert, Jung said, focuses his attention on the external world, on what goes on around him, while the introvert is more concerned with what goes on within him, in his inner psychic world. Thus the extrovert is more sociable and dependent upon others, whereas the introvert is more self-reliant and independent. Yet although the extreme extrovert is a back-slapping party type and the extreme introvert a moody loner, for the majority the difference is more one of attitude rather than behaviour.

49

1 If you choose perfumes with an oriental-floral fragrance, such as Must de Cartier, Oscar de la Renta,

Jicky, KL, Anais Anais, Poison, L'Air du Temps, etc., this identifies you as an introvert with changing or unstable moods. Hence you have a greater psychic sensitivity and are more easily hurt than are those who prefer other perfume types.

2 If your favourite scents belong to the aldehyde-floral or balsomic fragrance group, such as Chanel No. 5, Madame Rochas, White Linen, Arpège, Tuxedo, Rive Gauche, etc., then you are an introvert with steady moods. You are therefore more stable than the introvert type mentioned above.

3 If you prefer one of the heavier-scented perfumes, such as Opium, Coco, Obsession, Youth Dew and Loulou which have a floral-fruity fragrance, this identifies you as an extrovert with changing moods. Others won't always know where they are with you, although your down periods are more likely to upset yourself.

4 But should your perfume taste run to those with a lighter chypre fragrance, like Intimate, Ma Griffe, Miss Dior, Volcan d'Amour, Diva, Senchal, etc., then you are an extrovert with steady moods. It takes a lot to get you down and others probably regard you as a 'good old dependable'.

Our sense of smell, however, is greatly inferior to that possessed by most other mammals. But we have good vision, and we are doubly fortunate in being able to see colours, which gives our world a richness that is denied to those animals like dogs and cats, which are colour blind. But we are not the only animals that can see colours. Both birds and bees, for example, have colour vision, and indeed the nineteenth-century scientist Sir John Lubbock showed that bees are most attracted to blue, the colour of favourite bee flowers like borage and lavender, and least to red. In this respect bees resemble ourselves, as blue always tops the colour popularity stakes with us humans, while red comes at the bottom.

It has long been known that certain colours have a striking effect on our physiology and mood, and thereby affect our behaviour. For example, red has been found to increase appetite and hurry people up, and it has been put to good use by the sharper restaurateur both to get customers to eat more and to increase table turnover. Blue generally has a calming effect and has proved useful in changing people's minds about committing suicide, which is why many bridges, such as London's Blackfriars Bridge, have been painted blue to deter would-be suicides. And bubble-gum pink, which is also known as 'passive pink', has been widely used in the United States to calm down violent prisoners and mental asylum inmates.

Just as colours can influence our mood and behaviour, so they can in turn reveal our personality. Indeed, your favourite colour is a reliable guide to the sort of person that you are. So check which one of the following colours is your favourite before reading on: red, orange, yellow, pink, blue, green, brown, violet, white, or black.

50

If your favourite colour is:

1 *Red:* you are an active, outgoing, passionate, energetic, and rather intense type, who likes to be noticed and to be, where possible, the centre of attention. You are direct and outspoken, although you hate to be criticised. You are also impetuous and impatient, characteristics that can get you into trouble if you're not careful, but cannot be faulted for your warmth and generosity.

2 *Orange:* you are similar in many ways to the person who loves red, yet you are less self-centred and intense. You are basically a cheerful, optimistic and happy type, although you quickly become frustrated if your forward progress is impeded.

3 *Yellow:* you are lively and young-at-heart, with a good sense of humour and a ready wit. You enjoy talking

and listening to gossip, yet despite this you are not as shallow as you sometimes seem. Indeed, you have an inquisitive mind and a retentive memory. But you can be critical of others, and you may be vindictive if you are crossed or let down. You enjoy change and variety, and you love to travel.

4 *Pink:* you are a rather shy and insecure person, which is why you are easily hurt and upset. You try to get on with everyone, as you like a peaceful life, and you go out of your way to avoid arguments. But when you have the loving support of a partner or friends, you can overcome your natural diffidence and exploit your artistic talents and your adaptability.

5 *Blue:* you are a sensitive, decent, easy-going, and orderly person, yet because you tend to keep your emotions under fairly tight control, you often give the impression of being cold and unfeeling. You have conservative views that make you somewhat backward-looking and old-fashioned. Your loyalty and trustworthiness make you a dependable employee.

6 *Green:* you are quiet and tolerant, yet you know your own mind and you won't be hurried into doing anything. But you dislike upsets and arguments, and will always try to reach a compromise. Your horror of scandal is one reason why you try to live honestly and decently. You are loyal to your friends and to your principles.

7 *Brown:* you have much in common with the green-loving person, particulary in your desire to make haste slowly, although you are more pessimistic and also prone to depression. You like working with your hands, and indeed you may well have artistic talents. You are slow to anger, but once aroused, you can be violent.

8 *Violet:* you place a great importance on personal freedom, as you hate to be tied down or made to obey another's rules. In fact you dislike responsibility, which stems from your refusal to grow up. Your lack

of foresight hinders you in planning ahead, and this makes you vulnerable when things go wrong. You are also vain. But your brightness and exuberance can bring you a lot of social success.

9 *White:* white consists of undifferentiated spectral colours, which is why you are something of a wolf in sheep's clothing. For while you outwardly appear cool, calm and collected, your persona masks deep passions and strongly held convictions. You are even prepared to fight for what you believe, but because you are a hypocrite, you don't always dance to your own tune. And although you seem distant and unapproachable, your are really quite warm once contact has been made.

10 *Black:* black is not a colour; rather, it is the absence of colour, and it reveals you to be a sophisticated and worldly person, or at least as someone who would like to have these qualities, and not one who is preoccupied with death. Your aloofness is an expression of your insecurity; you also lack strong emotions. You enjoy mystifying others, and you may pretend to support ideas that you actually dislike, or you may live in a world of fantasy.

When we decorate our homes, our chief concern is to use colours that complement our personality and improve our mood. But we have no choice over what colours are used at our work, although many employers are becoming aware of the importance of these. Certain colours are oppressive and can lower efficiency, while others boost worker moral and output. A study carried out in Boston among office workers found that 72 per cent preferred cool blues and greens, of which pastel shades were the most popular. Pale yellow also received a lot of votes. Only 10 per cent of the sample opted for grey.

Researchers have also discovered that the colour of pills and tablets can either hasten or retard the recovery from the illness for which the medication they contain is prescribed.

A 1970 study carried out by Dr Kurt Schapira at Newcastle-upon-Tyne, for example, plotted the effects of the same drug administered as either green, yellow or red pills to psychiatric patients. Those suffering from acute anxiety recovered fastest when they were given green pills, whereas those with depressive symptoms responded best to yellow pills. Recovery was slowest among those patients who were given red-coloured pills. Yet where heart attack patients are concerned, it has been shown that red tablets are most effective in speeding recovery, presumably because red, being the colour of blood, suggests to the recipients that the drug contained in the tablets is right for their condition.

But now, if you are at home, or even in your office, take a look around and notice how the furniture is arranged. For example, are the chairs and tables positioned close to one another or are there wide spaces between them? Is everything neat and tidy or is there a certain amount of mess? And how many chairs stand around your dining room table? These and other features of your surroundings provide clues to your personality and how you choose to deal with the world.

51

Should the furniture of your living room or office be set apart, especially if it is arranged around the walls leaving a large central space, it reveals that you dislike closeness and human contact, which means that you are emotionally cool. But should the opposite be the case, with the furniture pieces grouped close together and any spaces between them filled with potted plants, or objects d'art, or even screens, then this layout shows you to be warmer and more welcoming. Hence you like contact with others.

Your kitchen speaks volumes about you, too. If yours resembles a hospital operating theatre in its sterility, wherein all the utensils are either placed out of sight or hung on the walls as ornaments, it not only says that you are emotionally cool but that you are disinterested in food and cooking. But if your kitchen has a homelier character and a more practical layout, then it reveals you to be a social type who likes both cooking and nurturing others. However, should your kitchen have a counter, or if it communicates with the dining room via a serving hatch (which you use), it shows that while you don't mind feeding people, you don't want to encourage intimacy.

Where the dining room is concerned, research has shown that those homes with a circular dining table are inhabited by more friendly and sociable families than those with either square or rectangular dining tables. And if your dining table is surrounded by several chairs positioned close together, it marks you as a hospitable type, whereas if there are only two or three chairs spaced widely apart, then you are an unwilling entertainer.

If you keep your cupboards very tidy it is a sign that you keep your emotions under tight control, and you may be neurotic if you fly into a tantrum if anything in them is disturbed. Moderately untidy cupboards suggest inner calm and a lack of neuroticism, but if your cupboards are the only untidy places in your home, it suggests that you are in the grip of long-standing psychological conflicts.

If you keep your bathroom like a Vogue show-room, then you are immature, but if it is messy and unsanitary, it shows you to be suffering from depression.

Black paintwork in the home is also a sign of depression, while if you have painted your doors and walls brown, it reveals that you have manic-depressive tendencies. A white-painted bedroom is indicative of frigidity, and one painted violet betokens sexual immaturity. Dull and drab colours in the home are evidence of a lack of warmth and spontaneity, whereas those that are bright and cheerful reveal opposite qualities.

It has long been said that we show our character by the way

that we laugh, and there is much truth in this. A warm, pleasant laugh invariably belongs to a warm and pleasant person, while the cold and unfeeling man or woman usually has a laugh of like quality.

But equally revealing is the type of joke or humorous situation that creates the laugh. In fact many psychologists now believe that our sense of humour reflects our personality, and recently a research team at Antioch College, California, designed a sense of humour test to get people laughing out their inner selves.

For instance, which of the following jokes—and each is representative of a different joke type—do you find the funniest?

1   A man fell from a high cliff but managed to grab hold of a tree root. Hanging in mid-air, he shouted out to Heaven: 'Is anyone up there?'
    A voice replied, 'Yes, my son. Let go of the root and I will bear thee up.'
    The man hesitated, glanced worriedly down, then cried out: 'Is anyone else up there?.

2   A blind man with a guide dog went into a department store, picked up the dog by its tail and swung it around his head. Seeing him, an assistant rushed over and said, 'May I help you, sir?'
    'No thanks,' the blind man replied, 'I'm just browsing.'

3   Q. How do elephants make love under water?
    A. They take their trunks off.

4   A prospective client asked a solicitor what his charges were and was told that it would cost him £40 for three questions.
    'Isn't that dreadfully expensive?' said the man.
    'Yes,' replied the solicitor, 'Now, what's your last question?'

5   Did you hear about the Irishman who couldn't understand why his sister had three brothers and he only had two?

6 Man to woman, while pouring her a drink:
   'Say when.'
   Woman: 'Right after this drink.'

7 A man drove quite properly through a green light,
   but as he did so a woman, driving an estate car con-
   taining 10 children, went through the red light and
   crashed into him.
   The man shouted: 'You stupid woman, don't you
   know when to stop?'
   'Oh,' she replied, 'they're not all mine!'

8 Puzzled doctor to patient: 'Have you had this before?
   Patient: 'Yes.'
   Doctor: 'Well, you've got it again.'

You may well have had a good belly laugh at one of these
jokes, chuckled at two or three of them, but found the
remainder distinctly unfunny. This is not surprising, as each
falls into a different category of humour. No 1 is a philosophical joke; No 2 is a sick joke; No 3 is a nonsensical joke; No
4 is a social satire joke; No 5 is an ethnic joke; No 6 is a sexual joke; No 7 is a joke degrading to women, and No 8 is
a hostile joke. The joke type you laughed hardest at reveals
your personality.

52

1 **The philosophical joke:** if this joke tickles you the
   most it brands you as a naturally cheerful, alert,
   enthusiastic, expressive, yet somewhat impulsive person. You feel secure with your belief system, and are
   thus able to laugh at both yourself and the human
   condition. Psychologists would say that you probably
   have the healthiest sense of humour.

2 **The sick joke:** if this is your favourite type of joke
   you have much in common with the philosophical
   joke person, in that you are cheerful, enthusiastic,
   and impulsive, but also frank and outgoing. And contrary to what might be expected, you are not insensitive to the sufferings and misfortunes of others.

3 **The nonsensical joke:** if you split your sides at this kind of joke it reveals that you are self-assured, with a placid, optimistic, calm and resilient demeanour. You are alert to incongruity, which means that you can find something to laugh about in almost any situation.

4 **The social satire joke:** if this is your idea of humour you are unconventional, with a good imagination and plenty of ideas. But you are also stubborn, irritable, suspicious, and somewhat superior. At worst, you can be jealous and overbearing.

5 **The ethnic joke:** if you crack up at this type of joke it reveals that you are cynical, unsentimental, and pretty tough-minded. You probably think that many a true word is spoken in jest, which suggests that you feel somewhat superior to people of other lands.

6 **The sexual joke:** if you laugh loudest at sexual jokes that are neither hostile nor degrading, it shows you to be impulsive, generous, uninhibited, and unsophisticated.

7 **The degrading joke:** if you find jokes that make the opposite sex—or, indeed, members of your own sex—look stupid, then you are old-fashioned, image-conscious, and rather insecure. You have little sympathy for the weak or the underdog, and you tend to see things in cut and dried, black and white terms.

8 **The hostile joke:** the joke team at Antioch College found that 'overconventional males who want to live up to social expectations of being tough guys' tend to laugh at hostile jokes. Hence if this type of joke makes you curl up, it means that you're self-assured, self-confident, and resilient. It also takes a lot to sway your feelings.

But if you lack a sense of humour, maybe sport is more your thing. And even this is revealing, as researchers at the Université de Montréal, Québec, discovered recently. They examined the personality types of those who played golf, tennis, or swam, and of those who practised yoga. Each activity attracted a different type of person, and it emerged that those who played tennis had the best all-round characters.

53

If you're a golfer, the Université de Montréal team says that this means you're sociable, competitive, thoughtful, and somewhat aggressive, which they classify as positive characteristics, but that you are let down by your lack of spontaneity, poor discipline, and unwillingness to take risks.

Should tennis be your favourite sport, it show that you're likewise sociable, competitive, thoughtful, and fairly aggressive, but also spontaneous and willing to take risks, although like golfers, you are ill-disciplined.

If you're a swimmer, then you fare badly, being classified as unsociable, lacking in spontaneity and aggression, and seldom thoughtful, competitive, or willing to take risks.

And if you prefer yoga, then you are a person lacking in spontaneity, competitiveness, and aggression. You are also unsociable and seldom take risks. However, you are quite thoughtful and disciplined.

Finally, we must consider the quirk of having one's body tattooed. This strange practice is still popular, and a recent survey carried out in the United States found that some 9 per cent of American men and 1 per cent of American women have tattoos. The proportion is much higher, however, among certain special groups, like sailors, where up to 50 per cent of those concerned may be tattooed.

It is perhaps unfortunate that while the tattoos themselves can often be quite artistic, the psychological traits that led to them being commissioned are seldom very positive. In fact as long ago as the early 1860s the Italian criminologist Cesare Lombroso was 'struck by a characteristic that distinguished the honest soldier from his vicious comrade: the extent to which the latter was tattooed and the indecency of the designs that covered his body'.

Tattoos are generally confined to the arms, although the hands, chest, back, stomach, buttocks and thighs can all serve as the tattooist's canvas, and Lombroso records that one Italian rapist had the words 'Entra tutto', or 'It enters all', tattooed on his penis.

Men tend to prefer tattoos of dragons, skulls, hearts, eagles and other birds of prey, military badges, crosses, daggers, V-signs, etc., words like 'Love' and 'Hate', which are typically emblazoned respectively across the fingers of either hand, and the names of girlfriends and other loved ones. Tattoos of shaking hands are particularly popular among pederasts. Women, by contrast, are more keen on tattoos of roses, hearts, butterflies, and the like.

'For many young individuals, the tattoo is a pictorial quest for self-definition,' says psychiatrist Gerald W. Grunet, 'easing one's sense of inadequacy and isolation by saying "I know who I am, I belong." It offers a tangible promise of a final identity, the clarified picture of a diffused ego.'

54

The main difficulty with analysing tattoos is their permanence, for they reflect the psychological inadequacies of the person concerned at the time when they were made, which may undergo a positive change in subsequent years. This is why many people regret having been tattooed when they grow older.

But it is known that tattoos symbolize immaturity and a poor self-image at the time when they were drawn. One study, for instance, specifically links tattoos with insecurity and depression in adolescent boys, while the self-inflicted tattoos typically made by imprisoned youths reflect their boredom and the inner anger that they feel. When adolescent girls have themselves tattooed, it invariably means that they are emotionally disturbed.

Unhappy and inadequate young people often turn to crime or become involved with drugs and drink, or have violent dispositions, which is why the presence of tattoos can often warn of a disturbed mind. The tattooed may well outgrow their early insecurities, yet the wise man or woman will give the tattooed, particularly the heavily tattooed, a wide berth.

Chapter Seven

SEXUAL ATTRACTION

Lust, thro' some certain strainers well refin'd,
Is gentle love, and charms all womankind.

Men and women have been looking at each other, and lusting after each other, and falling in love, ever since Adam disported with Eve in the Garden of Eden. We take such reciprocal interest between the sexes to be normal and entirely understandable, even though we are often obliged to ask ourselves 'What does she see in him?' or 'What on earth does he find attractive about her?' We tell ourselves that 'opposites attract' and also that 'like attracts like', and when logic fails to account for the disparity, content ourselves with the comfortable explanation that Love is a Mystery.

Yet Professor Bull, the head of psychology at Glasgow College of Technology, claims that each of us knows exactly how attractive we are and says that we tend to pair up with those members of the opposite sex who have about the same attractiveness rating. This is just as well, as another study has shown that marriages between couples of similar attractiveness last much longer than between those whose attractiveness rating is very different. And yet sometimes where the latter are concerned, as we mentioned in Chapter Two, there is a successful trade-off, when an older, unattractive, but rich and powerful man marries a beautiful woman. This happened in the case of Carlo Ponti and Sophia Loren, and

Aristotle Onassis and Jackie Kennedy.

But more interesting from our point of view is the discovery that particular types of women attract particular types of men, and vice versa. Indeed, a study carried out by Professor Nancy Hirschberg at the University of Illinois found that there is a distinct personality difference between those men who are respectively fixated by large breasts, or large buttocks, or long legs. So ask yourself: are you a breast man, a buttock man, or a leg man?

55

After spending 10 years investigating the personalities of men who preferred certain female parts, Professor Hirschberg came to the conclusion, although she may have been somewhat biased, that of the three types, it is the leg men who are the nicest sort. The character sketches of each type are given below:

1 The lover of large breasts tends to be a vain, independent, extroverted show-off, who seldom thinks about anything other than himself and who is unwilling to help other people.
2 The lover of large buttocks, by contrast, tends to be an orderly, self-abasing type, who is guilt-ridden and socially dependent.
3 The lover of leggy women, however, tends to be friendly and socially active, and willing to help others out.

Hence if you're a leg man, give yourself a pat on the back.

Professor Hirschberg is now investigating what sort of women are attracted to what sort of men, and has thus far noted that fat women, in general, prefer fat men, and that women who regard themselves as swingers are tempted by wiry, skinny men.

However, she has determined that women with large

breasts often have similar personalities, as do those with large behinds, and those with shapely legs. Therefore if you're a woman physically endowed in one or other of these areas, you may like to read what Professor Hirschberg says about you.

56

1 Women with large breasts are impulsive, independent, adventurous, and undependable.
2 Women with large bottoms tend to be introverted, self-abasing, guilt-ridden, and socially inactive.
3 Women with long, well-shaped legs are usually friendly, outgoing, feminine, and keen to make a good impression.

Hence the character of each type is similar to that of the man who is attracted by them, which indicates that, where personality is concerned, like does attract like. It also means that, when you come across a woman with large breasts, or a large bottom, or long legs, her distinctiveness in that region not only reveals her character, but also that of the man she is with.

A survey carried out among female students at Butler University, Indianapolis, in the 1970s by psychologist Sally Beck showed that their ideal man was of medium height, had a large, but not overly large, chest, and had small buttocks. Only a few of the women questioned expressed an interest in muscle-bound, barrel-chested he-men.

Dr Beck also discovered that women with similar personality traits tended to be attracted to the same type of men, just as Professor Hirschberg had noted that men who liked women of a particular type were very much alike. In fact if you are a woman, you may recognize yourself in the character sketches given below.

57

1 If you prefer medium-sized men, then you are likely to be an orderly, domestic type of person.

2 If you go for big men, you are probably more athletic and less traditionally feminine than the woman who prefers medium-sized men.

3 If you love big-chested men, however, this identifies you as outgoing but lacking in self-reliance, hence you are somewhat dependent.

4 If men with small bottoms turn you on, it means that you are competitive, highly motivated, and emotionally mature.

5 If you find yourself attracted to small men, then you are likely to be reserved and to have a mother who went to college or university.

6 Should you like men with plump bottoms, it reveals that you are homely and quite traditional.

Dr Beck's research also showed that most men, or at least most male American college students, find medium-sized women with small breasts and small buttocks to be the most desirable.

Another survey carried out among students, this time at London University in 1970 by Professor Hans Eysenck, found that a girl's personality determines the age at which she loses her virginity. Female students who were outgoing or extroverted reported that they first had sex when they were about 17 years old, whereas the quieter, more introverted girl on average kept her virginity until she was about 19 years old. When he announced these not very surprising findings to the British Psychological Society, Professor Eysenck said: 'The idea of a permissive society is not a true picture. Extroverts make love earlier, have more partners, do it more often, and seek sexual variety in what some people call perversions.' Thus it seems that extrovert girls, and of course their partners, have the most fun.

Where lovemaking is concerned, Professor Margaret Gibbs and two colleagues at Fairleigh Dickinson University in New

Jersey, USA, report that self-image is a good clue to how passionate a person is. Apparently the most assertive and passionate lovers are those who are not very concerned about their image, while those 'who are. . .very concerned about their image are game players and the more possessive'.

But there are more clues to how one makes love than self-image, and none is surely more odd than the way in which one cuts the lawn. The discovery of the link between how people cut their lawn and their sexual attitudes and behaviour was made by the inimitable Dr David Lewis, a clinical psychologist, who was responsible for the research, reported in Chapter Three, that showed how a person's taste in sandwich fillings reveals his or her sexual nature. But odd though it is, it does give you the opportunity, the next time you're looking over the garden fence, of evaluating the bedroom style of your neighbour(s).

58

Dr Lewis identified six different types of lawn which accurately reflect both the character and the sexual habits of their tenders: the perfect lawn, the striped lawn, the messy lawn, the scruffy lawn, the weedy lawn, and the wild lawn.

1   **The Perfect Lawn**: this lawn is only achieved and maintained with a good deal of effort and care, and hence it betokens the man or woman who is quiet, thoughtful, self-controlled, and critical, and who, in like manner, aims for perfection between the sheets. Yet he or she is not entirely confident, and requires both praise and a sense of security before reaching his peak, when he becomes a fun-loving, affectionate lover who takes great pride in his bedroom skills.

2   **The Striped Lawn**: neat, regular stripes in a lawn are indicative of an aloof, private, and secretive nature, and thus reveal the person who keeps to himself and

does not kiss and tell. Yet he or she is a hot-blooded and passionate lover, who greatly enjoys savouring the delights of love.

3 **The Messy Lawn**: the person who only cuts and tends his (or her) lawn somewhat infrequently, so that it has a messy appearance, is uncertain of his attractiveness or desirability, which makes it hard for him to initiate sexual activity. He is vulnerable to criticism, which can adversely affect his sexual performance. Yet when he feels secure, he is both readily aroused and is an eager lover. Thus he needs encouragement to bring out the best in him.

4 **The Scruffy Lawn**: the owner of this lawn, which is distinguished by its bare patches, has much in common with the previous type. He (or she) enjoys sex and is a willing and active participant, yet he suffers from doubts about both his attractiveness and about the standard of his sexual performance. Again, he needs plenty of encouragement to bring him up to par.

5 **The Weedy Lawn**: the person who lets weeds grow in his (or her) lawn finds it difficult to show much enthusiasm for anything, especially details, and is a shy lover in bed, with little interest in variety or experimentation. The weedy lawn man or woman thus tends to be a rather conventional lover.

6 **The Wild Lawn**: the wild, overgrown lawn is more like a pasture field than a lawn, and it mirrors the oddball and unstable nature of its owner, whose attitude to sex is variable and confusing. Indeed, he or she is a person of extremes, sometimes avoiding sex altogether, but then becoming very demanding.

Of the 200 people interviewed by Dr Lewis, 20 per cent had perfect lawns, 20 per cent had striped lawns, 15 per cent messy lawns, 14 per cent scruffy lawns, 13 per cent weedy lawns, and 18 per cent wild lawns. So cheer up, you are not alone.

But regarding love rather than sex, are your needs normal and fulfilling, enabling you to both give and receive, or does your need for love outweigh your capacity to love? If the latter better describes you, you may have a craving for love, which may come to dominate your life almost like a craving for drugs. 'And no addiction is more agonizing than addiction to love,' says Dr George Seeds, a psychiatrist at the Southern California School of Medicine. 'The addict demands or begs that love be given to him or her—and that gradually escalates.' Such a situation is not only painful for the person concerned, but also for those who become the object of his or her affections.

At one extreme the love addict may conduct himself like a Don Juan, flitting from one affair to the next, breaking hearts but never giving his own, while at the other he may cling to one particular relationship, refusing to admit that it is over, sucking the life-blood of the partner like a modern-day Count Dracula. Between these two poles fall all manner of relationship situations, whose common denominator is a desperate need to be loved, and without which the addict feels bereft and unhappy and may be unable to function normally either at work or socially, or both.

Researchers at Metropolitan State College in Denver, Colorado, have compiled a check-list of symptoms which can help you determine if you have a problem in this area. They say that you may be a love addict if you have experienced three or four of them.

59

1 **Denial**. Your family and friends tell you that you're involved in a destructive relationship, but you disagree with them.
2 **Immediacy**. You require frequent and urgent discussions with your lover in social or business situations.
3 **Compulsion**. You've broken up 'for good' at least twice, yet you've always made up.
4 **Loss of control**. You often feel powerless to control

your feelings or behaviour with regard to your love.

5 **Progression**. As times goes by you suspect that your relationship is on a downward path.

6 **Withdrawal**. You become depressed and experience physical disturbances (loss of sleep, altered eating habits, etc.) when apart from your lover.

The causes of love addiction are complex and are as yet not fully understood. However, one underlying factor seems to be a poor self-image, something that often results from a lack of parental affection during the earliest years of life. Its treatment requires professional help, the addict being encouraged to both explore his cravings and to develop a control over them, but without denying his natural human desire for love and companionship.

Chapter Eight
BLOOD, SWEAT, AND FEET

'Yet Chloe sure was form'd without a spot'—
Nature in her then err'd not, but forgot.
'With ev'ry pleasing, ev'ry prudent part,
Say, what can Chloe want?'—She wants a Heart.

In the first chapter we discussed the four temperament types described by Hippocrates, namely the sanguine, the choleric, the melancholic, and the phlegmatic, which supposedly result from an imbalance of the four humours, these being blood, yellow bile, black bile, and phlegm. The sanguine person, for example, who is the most cheerful, outgoing, and intelligent of the four, has a surfeit of blood, the body fluid that is formed from the element Air.

Of the four humours, we are most familiar with, and most cognizant of, the properties of blood. Indeed, we never see either yellow bile or black bile, and phlegm is merely a rather disgusting slimy substance that we are all, on occasions, obliged to clear from our throats and noses. More familiar body liquids include tears, sweat, and urine, which largely fall into the waste-product category, and which lack the life-giving properties and the dramatic colour of blood.

Our blood, in fact, is vital to our existence. It transports food and oxygen to our tissues, and removes waste, such as carbon dioxide, from them. It carries hormones and distributes heat. It fights infection. And it clots to prevent its own loss, when the skin is wounded.

In 1901, two scientists, Stattock in England and Landsteiner in Germany, discovered that everyone's blood belongs to one of four groups, named A, B, AB, and O, which are distinguished by certain organic chemicals clinging to the red cells and by those floating in the plasma. This discovery explained why some blood transfusions had fatal consequences for the recipient.

In Britain, the largest number of people (about 45 per cent) have group O blood, with group A persons (about 43 per cent) coming a close second. Nine per cent of the population have group B blood, and the remaining 3 per cent have group AB blood. Those with AB blood are known as 'universal recipients' because they can receive blood from any of the groups without harmful consequences, while people with group O blood are called 'universal donors' as they can safely give blood to any of the groups. Yet group O people can only receive blood from group O donors, due to the fact that blood from any other group is fatal to them. In this respect they are somewhat unfortunate.

You are by now perhaps wondering what this has to do with character. Well, just as the four humours were once believed to produce the four character types described by Hippocrates, so the Japanese of today maintain with equal seriousness that each blood group is linked with specific character traits, thereby giving rise to the blood group A person, the blood group B person, the blood group AB person, and the blood group O person. Each has his (or her) own way of behaving, likes and dislikes, job preferences, social attitudes, reaction to stress, etc. In fact Japanese employers often demand to know the blood type of prospective employees, in order to ascertain if they are temperamentally suited for the vacant position. And different blood group types need handling differently. One Tokyo restaurant manager, for example, found that it didn't pay to criticize his blood group A employees. 'Before, things didn't go well,' he said. 'People would quit. But now I've begun dealing with workers according to their blood type, things are going great.'

Which means that, instead of asking people at parties what sign of the zodiac they were born under, a line of enquiry that is passé and all too obvious, equivalent information about their personality can be gained by discovering their blood group. But first, you may be interested to learn what your blood group says about you.

60

(1) **Blood Group A**: if you belong to this group you are rather uptight and tense, which makes you susceptible to stress and prone to irritability. In fact you find it difficult to relax. You have high standards and your own way of doing things, and your need to be always right can create problems for you in your relations with others. This explains why you dislike criticism or being told what to do. You are a perfectionist by nature, which enables you to cope with details and the nitty-gritty, but which makes it hard for you to know when to stop. As a boss you can become something of a slave driver, forcing those working under you to reach for impossible goals. Yet while you present yourself to the world as someone who knows what he wants and where he is going, you are basically quite shy and unsure of yourself, more introverted than outgoing. It is your lack of confidence that prompts you to seek security by trying to control what is happening around you. And it is also the reason why you function best when you have the loving support of a partner. But hardly surprisingly, you are prone to nervous disorders and to depression. You prefer those sports and games that are not too arduous and which allow you to demonstrate certain skills, such as chess, bridge, snooker, golf, badminton and squash. You are neat and clean, both inside and outside, and in this respect you are rather repressed. But while you have high standards, you are also inclined to be hypocritical. At your best you are creative, efficient, thorough, and totally honest; but when things are not going so well, you can be carping, argumentative, bad-tempered, and all too quick to blame somebody else for your mistakes.

(2) **Blood Group B**: if you have blood of this type you are an independent, freedom-loving person, who hates to be tied down or restricted in any way. This unfortunately means that you dislike responsibility and hence avoid commitment, so you cannot always be relied upon. You are best suited to either freelance occupations or to those that allow you considerable freedom of movement and action. You enjoy travel, especially to foreign parts. You possess a lot of self-confidence, and your natural enthusiasm and way with words gives you the ability to stimulate, influence and per-suade others. Indeed, you make a good salesman. But while you have these advantages, you tend to lack direction or clear-sighted goals and thus may waste your talents on fool-ish or unworthy schemes. You are also poor at handling money, which tends to slip through your fingers as soon as you get your hands on it, and you should avoid, where possible, any job that puts you in charge of the finances. Your sociable nature and friendly disposition make you generally popular, and you are blessed with an intuitive understanding of your fellow men and women. You dislike arguments and any form of upset and unpleasantness, although you are inclined to bring these down upon your own head by your irresponsible behaviour. You are quite creative, and enjoy writing, drama, and the arts.

(3) **Blood group AB**: if you have this blood group you belong to an exclusive fraternity, one that you share with only 3 per cent of the population. You are fortunate in being a well-balanced and stable person, with steady, sensible views on life and love. Hence perhaps not surprisingly, you are polite and reserved, disliking ostentation and unruly behaviour. You are fair and honest, and have a strong sense of right and wrong, attitudes that incline you towards the law, community work, and trade union activities. You also have a good brain and enjoy studying, yet because you prefer to specialize you may lack a broad understanding of your chosen field. You are not averse to expressing criticism when you feel that it is deserved, and your objectivity and absence of bias makes you a good adjudicator or mediator. Your chief

fault is vacillation, which mainly affects you in any situation where your emotions are involved. This is why you find it hard to end a love relationship that has gone sour for you.

(4) **Blood group O**: if you have this blood group, it identifies you as a careful and cautious person, who likes to be in control and to know where you are going. Yet this does not mean that you are a boring stick-in-the-mud, as you are prepared to take risks that are calculated and to make excursions that are either financially or spiritually rewarding. You are ambitious, yet you are blessed with the virtue of patience, which means that you are capable of working long and hard to get what you want. In this respect you are a bit like a bulldog, never prepared to let go. Few things daunt you, always providing that you have the opportunity to plan ahead and work out your moves. While you are naturally prudent, you hate the idea of money lying idly around, which is why you prefer to invest any spare cash in property or land, which can bring you a safe return. Where others are concerned you are normally open and friendly, although you do need time to think and be alone, as you have an introspective side. Your discriminating taste helps you to be a good buyer and enables you to dress both stylishly and with flair. You make a loyal and dutiful marriage partner, although your strong sexual urge can tempt you into having an affair. But if the opposite happens, and you are betrayed by your lover or spouse, you find it very hard to either understand or forgive. Indeed, you can be quite malicious and hurtful at times, and although you rarely show this side of yourself, it can shock those who know you when brought into the light of day.

We fortunately rarely see blood unless we accidentally cut ourselves, although its presence within the blood vessels of the skin is revealed by the pinkish hue that it imparts to our complexion. But if blood is a liquid of our interior selves, sweat, by contrast, is one of our exterior selves, flowing outwards as it does from the skin pores, to bathe our skin and

so cool our bodies by evaporation. It also helps to remove
wastes from the body. Indeed, sweat contains urea and
mineral salts, and is in many ways very much like the urine
that we void from our bladders.

But while sweating is normally a response to an increas-
ing body temperature, it is also linked with our emotional
state, and any negative emotion from agitation to extremes
of terror can produce the 'cold sweat' so beloved of horror
film makers. And there are some people who sweat a lot
but who are neither hot nor terrified, a condition which
results from their own inner anxiety, as mentioned below.

The miraculous 'sweating' of statues and other non-living
objects has from time to time been reported and cannot
always be so easily explained away by assuming that the
'sweat' is condensed water vapour from the air. In classical
times such happenings were regarded as omens, whose
meaning reflected the outcome of some important event of
the day. For example, Plutarch tells us that when Alexander
the Great was preparing to invade Asia a statue of Orpheus
at Libethra in Thrace, which was made of cypress wood,
sweated profusely for several days. Many were alarmed by
this prodigy, but the seer Aristander took a far more positive view, saying that 'it signified that Alexander would perform actions so worthy to be celebrated, that they would
cost the poets and musicians much labour and sweat'. And
as it turned out, he was quite right. Yet when the statue of
Mark Anthony at Alba began sweating prior to his battle with
the army of Augustus Caesar, it was obvious to all that
Anthony was destined to be defeated. And indeed he was.

61

If you have hands that are dry, without being cracked or
rough, then your emotions are stable. But if they are moist
it reveals that you are suffering from inner anxiety, while
if they are very moist and clammy, as was mentioned in an
earlier chapter, then you are chronically nervous and suffer
from a low self-esteem. If you have hands that are cold, white

and moist, but have nothing physically wrong with you, they indicate that you are either very depressed or are suffering from a psychotic condition. And should your hands sweat very quickly when your emotions are aroused, they show you to be emotionally unstable. Such instability is also revealed when the sweating affects the entire body, a phenomenon jocularly known as *hyperpersperiasis*.

Sweat left unattended can result in body odour, and those who neglect personal hygiene in this regard are often self-absorbed, hypocritical, and contentious, qualities that result from a poor self-image. In fact smelly people tend to reproduce in their malodorousness the subconsciously acquired belief that they are 'bad' or 'rotten'. Indifferent oral hygiene likewise results in bad breath. The philosopher Aristotle was hard on those who suffered from this complaint. He wrote, 'He whose mouth smells of a bad breath is one of a corrupted liver and lungs, is oftentimes vain, wanton, deceitful, of indifferent intellects, envious, covetous, and a promise breaker.' His opinion should be sufficient to persuade you to gargle at least once a day.

The feet also require careful attention to prevent them from publicly announcing their presence. Feet that are studiously neglected, so allowing them to smell, are symptomatic of inner disquiet, whereas sweet-smelling feet, if there are such things, betoken a far more stable and healthy psychological state.

Nowadays feet suffer from the disadvantage of being largely hidden from view, which prevents them from being studied by anyone except their owner and his or her chiropodist. This is unfortunate because feet are just as informative about character and fate as the hands. In fact it is now time for you to remove your shoes and socks (or stockings) and take a long look at your own.

62

It is a well-known folk belief that large feet in a man signify his ownership of a large phallus, whereas small feet suggest the contrary. The same thing is also said about large and small noses. However, the author knows of no scientific study correlating foot size with penis size, which means that only those male readers with either large or small feet will know the real truth.

According to Aristotle, if your feet are broad and long and fleshy, with skin that feels firm to the touch, they show that you have a big appetite and a strong constitution, but are somewhat lacking in brain power. But if your feet are narrow and lean and have a soft skin, then while you are both physically and constitutionally weak, you are blessed with a clever mind. If the skin of the soles of your feet is very thick, it reveals that you are strong, confident and bold, whereas if it is thin, it shows that you are physically weak, shy and cowardly.

Your toes by themselves can give you an insight into your character and fate. The ideal toes are long, straight, shapely, and set close together, and as such they reflect positive qualities of character and a fortunate life. Indeed, long, straight toes betoken a long life.

The big toes, like the thumbs, are representative of willpower and personal force, and if yours are large and well-shaped they indicate that you are richly endowed in these respects. Contrariwise, should your big toes be small or thin or bent, or generally under-sized, then you have some lack of these qualities.

If you are a man it is fortunate if your second toes have square ends and exceed your big toes in length, as they indicate that you will have a happy and fulfilling life. But should you be a woman such toes reveal that you are bossy and sexually promiscuous, and suggest that you will therefore have a troubled marriage. The criminologist Cesare Lombroso noted that many prostitutes have a wide space between the big toe and the second toe of their feet, which

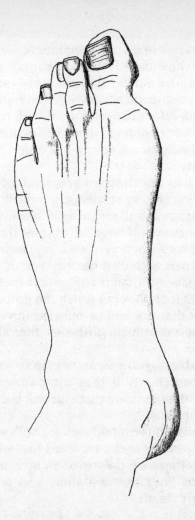

Figure 27: Foot with large big toe and shorter second toe

is often developed to such an extent that the toes are quasi-prehensile. If your second toes are shorter than your big toes, they portend both a troubled and a short life. When the second toes equal the big toes in length they represent rather bland life circumstances, with few highs or lows.

Again, if you are a man and have third toes that are longer than your second toes, such a feature reveals that you may become a widower. But if your third toes equal your second toes in length, they identify you as a lucky person, who always comes up trumps in the end. Very long third toes mark you out as someone who will find it hard to gain any recognition in life. If you are a woman with third toes that are longer than your big toes, then you are not only unfortunate but are likely to cause other people a lot of annoyance and anxiety.

Long fourth toes are the sign of a studious nature and hence promise success in academic pursuits. Short fourth toes, however, are not at all fortunate in meaning. For example, if you are a man and have fourth toes that are shorter than your third toes, then you are a philanderer, whereas if you are a woman such toes identify you as an argumentative trouble-maker. Indian tradition says that if the fourth toe of a woman's foot does not touch the ground when she walks, it means that she will be married three times. Yet if she has both short fourth and fifth toes, then she is unlikely to marry at all.

It is a favourable sign if you are a man to have long little or fifth toes, particularly if they are partnered by broad second toes, as they indicate that you will become wealthy and lead a happy life.

Thin toes are an unfortunate sign for both sexes because they represent poverty and a troubled life, while toes that are twisted or otherwise deformed signify an untruthful, deceitful nature. Toes that are short and widely spaced betoken an early death.

Where other people are concerned we are far more likely to see their shoes than their bare feet. But even this can be revealing, because the shoes themselves, according to psychologist Dr David Hewitt, reflect the inner man or woman.

63

First, the shoe types worn by women:

1 **Stilettos**: the wearer is more interested in partying and having fun with the opposite sex than in improving her mind. In fact she does not want to be taken seriously. And because she tends to be thoughtless and irresponsible, she cannot be relied upon or depended upon. Yet in her limited way, she is lively and energetic.

2 **Suede pumps or flatties**: these are worn by the woman who is independent and practical, and who takes herself fairly seriously. She has strong, forthright views, and she prides herself on her reliability. She does not slavishly follow fashion, but likes to appear in something striking.

3 **Calf-length boots**: these reveal that the wearer is clinging to her childhood. She presents herself as an authoritarian person with a no-nonsense, superior attitude, yet she is often passionate but frustrated inside. However, she is a good organizer with a flair for leadership.

4 **Flat, chunky shoes**: such shoes are worn by the busy, practical, conventional woman with no time for the vagaries of fashion or for fripperies. She tends to be bossy and outspoken. She has no patience with foolish or irresponsible people.

5 **Low-heeled court shoes**: these are worn by the reliable, self-controlled but somewhat conventional woman, who wants to be feminine but who can't afford to be thought too sexy or lightweight. Yet she can turn into a sex-pot behind closed doors.

6 **Slingbacks**: this woman is glitzy and likes wealth and show. She is likely to be ambitious and to have a sharp brain. Her tongue is sharp too.

Next, the shoes worn by men and their meaning.

1 **Brogues**: these are favoured by solid, dependable

men, who have old-fashioned values and ways of behaviour. But although they are strong on honesty and doing the right thing, they are often shy about revealing their real feelings. Hence they are touched with hypocrisy.

2 **Casual slip-ons**: this man either lives, or wants to give the impression that he lives, a life of self-indulgent luxury. Yet at base he is flippant and irresponsible. He may even play golf.

3 **Trainers**: these are worn by the young, spunky and immature person, who loves to thumb his nose at authority. His principal interest is to cut a cool figure with those he considers to be the 'in' crowd.

4 **Open-toed sandals**: these are favoured by passive, ozone-friendly, alternative men, who are happiest doing the washing up and looking after the kids while their partners are out bringing home the bacon. Their feet are stuck in the magical year of 1967, when they think the world became a temporary paradise.

5 **Doc Martens**: once worn by working-class yobbos, these have now been adopted by caring, sensitive, style-conscious, middle-class neo-wimps.

6 **Cowboy boots**: it is very odd when an urban male wears cowboy boots, for while he wants to give the impression that he is at home on the range, he is more likely to be a mixed-up poseur. And be warned, cowboy boot wearers often have strange sexual hang-ups.

If the above discourse on the meaning of feet and shoes has put a smile on your face, you may be interested to know that the ancients, according to the essayist Joseph Addison, referred to this particular humorous expression as the Ionic laugh, which he tells us 'is for the most part confined to the fair sex, and their male retinue'. The smirk or simper, which is typically productive of dimples, was called the Chian laugh, whereas the plain grin was known as the Syncrusian laugh, and the sneering grin as the Megaric laugh.

'I shall range all old amorous dotards under the denomination of Grinners,' Addison tells us; 'when a young blooming wench touches their fancy, by an endeavour to recall youth to their cheeks, they immediately overstrain their muscular features, and shrivel their countenance into this fright-

Figure 28: Phillip Schofield demonstrating his version of the Ionic laugh

ful merriment.' The ordinary laugh was termed a Risus laugh, and the guffaw or coarse laugh was called the Sardonic laugh. 'Punsters, I find, very much contribute towards the Sardonic,' notes Addison, 'and the extremes of either wit or folly seldom fail of raising this noisy kind of applause. As the ancient physicians held the Sardonic laugh very beneficial to the lungs, I should, methinks, advise all my countrymen of consumptive and hectical constitutions to associate with the most facetious punsters of the age.'

The efficacy of both smiles and laughter in uplifting our mood and benefiting our health work by their cooling action on the brain, says Dr Robert B. Zajonc, professor of psychology at the University of Michigan and the academic who rediscovered the ideas of Israel Waynbaum, which the latter gave to the world in his book *Physionomie humaine: son mécanisme et son rôle social*, published in 1907 (see Chapter Two). 'The temperature of the brain dictates changes in emotional reactions,' claims Zajonc. 'The brain generally works more comfortably when it is cool. When it overheats it produces negative feelings and tetchiness.'

Our moods are governed by the hypothalamus of the brain. And apparently smiling and laughing, as well as actions like pen-chewing, nail-biting, and yawning, cause us to breathe more deeply. This allows more heat to be lost from the network of blood vessels under the hypothalamus, thereby cooling this important area and so beneficially influencing our mood. Sombre expressions, on the other hand, like pouting and grimacing, constrict the nostrils and reduce the breathing rate, which in turn hinders the cooling of the hypothalamus. This brings about a worsening of our mood, so causing gloomier expressions and thus starting a cycle of despondency. The key to breaking this cycle is simply to force yourself consciously to smile or laugh, or to breathe deeply—or of course you can make someone give you a jolly good tickle.

Chapter Nine

ANIMALS, ORPHANS, AND LITTLE PEOPLE

I am his Highness' dog at Kew;
Pray tell me, sir, whose dog are you?

We humans are the only creatures that form symbiotic relationships with other animals, which we tame either to work for us or to be our domestic pets. No one knows when or by whom the first horse was harnessed and ridden, or when or how the domestic cat and dog were bred, yet our earliest written records tell us that these animals, and others, were important members of ancient societies; indeed, those societies could not have existed without them.

The Egyptians, for example, held animals in the highest esteem, believing them to be sacred. 'Anyone who deliberately kills one of these animals', records Herodotus, writing of the Egyptians' attitudes to both tame and wild animals, 'is punished by death; should one be killed accidentally, the penalty is whatever the priests choose to impose; but for killing an ibis or a hawk, whether deliberately or not, the penalty is inevitably death.'

It is well-known that the Egyptians loved cats, but they were equally fond of dogs. And the death of the family pet, whether a dog or a cat, was an occasion of deepest mourning. 'All the inmates of a house where a cat has died a natural death shave their eyebrows,' says Herodotus, 'and when a dog dies they shave the whole body including the head. Cats which have died are taken to Bubastis, where they are embalmed and buried in sacred receptacles; the dogs are buried, also in sacred places, in the towns where they belong.'

Alexander the Great so loved his dog Peritas and his horse Bucephalus that when they died he founded a city to honour each of them, naming one Peritas and the other Bucephale.

In modern Britain, as in most of the civilized world, cats and dogs are the most popular pets. You may own one or the other, or both, yourself. If so, you will be interested to know that your choice in this respect says quite a lot about you as a person.

A number of studies have shown that there are distinct differences between those people who prefer cats to dogs and those who prefer dogs to cats, which are greatest between the cat owner who actually dislikes dogs and the dog owner who dislikes cats. The two animals in question are very different in themselves, and a strong preference for one of them is believed to reflect their human admirer's recognition of, and positive response to, the character qualities they display. Cats, for instance, are independent and emotionally cool animals, whereas dogs are essentially sociable and warm-hearted. Hence if you own a dog or a cat your character tends to resemble that of your pet.

64

If you are a cat owner you are likely to be an independent type of person; hence freedom of thought and action are important to you. You avoid getting bogged down with responsibilities, and you are not all that keen on emotional ties. In fact, like the cat, you are emotionally restrained. You are essentially an introverted, thinking type, dealing with the world by carefully planning your moves and then moving in quickly to snatch what you want. Your life strategy is based on patience and stealth, and when confronted by opposing forces you will try to outwit them instead of tackling them head on. Yet while you lack martial courage, and dislike making a noise or creating a scene, you can usually avoid difficulties if you have enough time to plan your moves. You enjoy discovering inner and deeper meaning, thus you are always looking beneath the surface of things to find out how they work. You probably have only a few friends, yet your relationship with them will be close, if not particularly warm.

However, if your are a dog owner, then your basic character is quite different. Like the pet of your choice, you have an open, friendly disposition, perhaps to the extent that you wear your heart on your sleeve. Because you enjoy being with others, you make a good team member and family ties are important to you, and indeed life would be empty for you if you were deprived of company. You prefer things to be up-front and out in the open, as you dislike deviousness and dissimulation. You are more extroverted, which implies that you are not much interested in what is going on beneath the surface, but tend to accept things at their face value. When moved or deeply touched, you display your feelings, and when you have something to say, you often blurt it out without stopping to think of the effect it might have on others. Lacking the subterfuge of the cat person, you tackle problems by dealing with them directly. You are generous and have a real concern for the plight of others, which can sometimes have you reaching deep into your pockets to help a worthy cause. In fact, perhaps not surprisingly, you stand up for the underdog, cheer the loser, and cry justice for the oppressed.

But not every pet owner enjoys the same type of relationship with his or her pet, and indeed the Pet Food Institute of America has discovered that there are five kinds of dog people and three types of cat people. If you are a dog owner or a cat owner you may be able to spot the category to which you belong.

65

The five dog types are:

1 **The Dog's Best Friend**: this group forms 27 per cent

of the dog-owning fraternity. They are very close to their pooch, whom they regard as a companion and as a family member.

2 **The Platonic Partners**: these enjoy having a dog but are not too close to it emotionally or psychologically. Some 17 per cent of dog owners belong to this group.

3 **The Crown Jeweller:** these are people who keep a dog essentially for show. They treat their pet, which is usually a pedigree dog, as if it were a piece of bone china and thus do not derive any real emotional satisfaction from it. The group makes up 13 per cent of dog owners.

4 **The Paperchasers**: these people can never feel relaxed with their dog because they are constantly worried that it may do something to distress or embarrass them. Such anxiety prevents a close bond developing between them and the mutt. Paperchasers make up 24 per cent of dog owners.

5 **The Dog Tired**: this group of dog owners resent their dog and hate having to feed and walk it. They found out the hard way that children never keep their promise to look after their pets. Nineteen per cent of dog owners are 'dog tired'.

The following are the three categories (no pun intended) of cat people:

1 **The Mirror Images**: these people recognize themselves in their cats and look after the animals as they do themselves. This 21 per cent group of cat owners are the only ones who really love moggies.

2 **The Strangers in the Night**: this is the largest group of cat owners, making up 59 per cent of the total. They are not really involved with their cats, but admire them for their independent spirit and for the fact that they don't require much looking after.

3 **The Litter Lovers**: these are people who look to their cats for love and affection, which they can't find elsewhere, and who, when the animal dies or goes miss-

ing, are left totally bereft. They make up 20 per cent of cat owners.

But what is it that attracts a person to one pet rather then another? Certainly the most popular pets are furry and responsive, such as dogs, cats, rabbits, etc., although plenty that are not, like fish, have a big following.

Astrologers say that our choice of pet is influenced by our zodiac sign of birth, For example, the astrologers of ancient India claimed that anyone's need for pets is determined by the quadruplicity of his or her birth.

The quadruplicity having the greatest liking for pets is made up of the so-called animals signs, these being Gemini, Virgo, Sagittarius, and Pisces. If you were born under one of these signs you are a tender and loving pet owner.

The second Indian quadruplicity consists of Taurus, Leo, Scorpio, and Aquarius. Because these are known as the vegetable signs, those born under them are less interested in owning pets than the sign types mentioned above. However, if you were born under one of these signs you can take pride in your love for, and your skill with, plants. You have a green thumb.

The last quadruplicity is made up of the mineral signs of Aries, Cancer, Libra, and Capricorn. The Indians believed such people to have the least interest in animals. Thus if you were born under one of these signs it accounts for your reluctance to own a pet—or your indifferent ownership of it if you do.

More specifically, a person's pet preferences often reflect the nature of his or her sign animal.

Gemini, Virgo and Aquarius are known as human signs because their sign creatures are human beings. For this reason they are also called bipedal signs. Libra is likewise classified as a human sign, despite its sign symbol being the Balance. Those born under these signs tend to like pets with two legs, such as birds, gerbils, and monkeys.

Aries, Taurus and Leo, whose sign animals are the Ram, the Bull, and the Lion, are referred to as quadrupedal signs.

Those born under them normally prefer pets with four legs and which are mammalian like their sign animals, e.g., dogs, cats, rabbits, guinea pigs, etc.

Sagittarius is a mixed sign, half-man and half-horse, as its sign animal is the Centaur. For this reason Sagittarians like both two-legged and four-legged animals, although they are particularly fond of horses.

Capricorn is also a mixed sign, half-goat and half-fish, its sign animal being the Sea Goat. Thus Capricorn natives like both fish and four-legged animals.

Those born under Cancer and Pisces, the signs of the Crab and the Fishes, enjoy keeping fish and maintaining aquatic environments.

Scorpio, whose sign animal is the Scorpion, is known as a crawling animal sign. Hence the Scorpio-born are attracted to scorpions, insects and other invertebrates, and also to reptiles and nocturnal animals.

If you are an Aries you may not be a great pet lover, but you are attracted, like the Sagittarius-born, to horses, which is fortunate for you as one of your lucky animals is the horse. Your other lucky animals, although they could not be safely kept in the average home, are the ram, the wolf, the leopard, the bear, and the owl.

If Taurus is your star-sign you will enjoy keeping four-legged animals, particularly dogs. You are not so keen, however, on cats. Your lucky animals are the cow, the camel, and the lynx. Pigeons are also very fortunate for you.

If you are a typical Gemini you will be fond of animals, and quite possibly you have one or more dogs. You also like birds. Indeed, parrots and linnets are lucky for you. Your other lucky animals are the ape, the bear, the fox, and the snake.

Although Cancer natives have an affinity for fish, they also like furry animals such as dogs, rabbits, and horses. If you were born under this sign you may well agree that you aren't all that fond of pets, particularly those that are messy and troublesome. You also aren't very keen on cats. But hardly surprisingly, your lucky animals are the seal, the turtle, and the otter, as well as the dog and the owl.

If you were born under Leo you are attracted to four-legged animals, especially dogs, cats and horses. You will, however, tend to prefer cats to dogs. You also may well like certain birds, such as the parrot and the mynah, and some fish. Indeed, the eagle, the cockerel, and the sparrow-hawk are lucky for you.

You're the ideal pet owner if you're Virgo-born, as you have a great liking, and sympathy, for animals. Apes and monkeys are particularly lucky for you, which is not surprising as Virgo is a human sign. Your other lucky animals include the fox, the squirrel, the snake, the parrot, the swallow, and the magpie.

You may well own a pet if you're a Libra. And if you do it is likely to be something small like a hamster, mouse, or guinea pig because you prefer small animals if they don't have two legs. Your lucky animals are the rabbit and the tortoise, and also the dove and the pigeon.

Tradition says that you prefer small animals too if you're a Scorpio, especially if they crawl! However, mice and reptiles are among your favourite pets. Some of your lucky animals are small and crawl, such as the scarab, the scorpion, and the lobster, but most are not. The latter include the horse, the wolf, the bear, and the panther.

If you are a Sagittarian native you will almost certainly be very fond of animals and probably have at least one pet. You favour dogs and horses, which are lucky for you, as are lions. You don't much like birds, although the peacock, the stork, the eagle, and the cuckoo, are likewise lucky for you. So too is the bull.

It perhaps won't surprise you to learn if you're a Capricorn that one of your lucky animals is the crocodile, which is four-legged and lives in water. Goats and donkeys are also fortunate for you, as are birds like the owl and the crow. And while you like cats and small dogs, you hate snakes and other reptiles.

You rather like exotic pets if you're an Aquarian, although few of them are practical to keep. Big dogs of unusual breeds, lions, tigers, and birds like macaws fascinate you, yet you tend to make a rather indifferent owner of any animals that you have. You also dislike being tied down by them. Your lucky animals are the dog, the squirrel, the eagle, and the peacock.

You are fond of pets if you're a Pisces, especially fish and other aquatic creatures, and you prefer animals that are not too much trouble to look after. Hence it is perhaps ironic that your lucky animals are the sheep, the ox, the swan, the stork, and the peacock.

It is of course true that many pets are bought by parents to satisfy their children's demands in this respect, and indeed those children who are not so indulged miss out on a unique and rewarding experience. Such lack of animal closeness may be one of the factors contributing to the urgent need shown by many emotionally deprived people to get ahead and make something of their lives, for according to Dr Pierre Rentchnik, a Swiss medical researcher, many historical leaders were either orphans, abandoned or illegitimate children, or were rejected by their fathers.

'A distinctive characteristic of the childhood of these leaders is the feeling of "nothing" or agonizing emptiness,' says Dr Rentchnik. 'The orphan in search of security becomes aggressive and tries to dominate society and destiny.'

Among the better-known Roman emperors, for example, were Caligula and Nero, whose fathers died when they were aged seven and three respectively. The mothers of both were banished, and the boys were brought up by relatives. Each not only rose to supreme power, but behaved with gross cruelty and immorality. Similarly, the emperor Augustus lost his father at age four, Tiberius his at age nine, and the father of Claudius died while he was still in the womb. Vespasian was also orphaned, and was raised by his paternal grandfather.

The modern leaders Atatürk, Lenin, Stalin and Hitler were either orphaned or lost their fathers before they reached the age of 15, and Winston Churchill, Mao Tse-tung, Gamal Nasser, Richard Nixon, Josif Tito, and Golda Meir were either rejected by their fathers or abandoned by them.

But if being orphaned or abandoned by your father is one clue as to how you might subsequently lead your life and to the type of person you might become, of more relevance for most people is the birth position that they occupied in their family. So are you a first-born or an only child, a middle child, or the baby of the family? Psychologist Kevin Leman of Tucson, Arizona has made a special study of the birth order syndrome and has concluded that 'the order in which children are born into a family is a powerful determinant of personality. It can influence the type of occupation they choose, how successful they are at it, the kind of people they marry and even the kind of parents they will be.'

66

First-born children tend to get the most attention from their parents, while of course only children get it all. They also bear the brunt of parental discipline and are under the strongest pressure not only to behave in an adult manner, but to perform well in all aspects of their lives. This means that if you are the first-born or the only child in your family, you are likely to be serious, cautious, conscientious, and reliable, as well as being something of a nitpicker, characteristics that help you keep your nose to the grindstone and thus make something of your life. For example, 52 per cent of American presidents were first-born sons, as were all seven astronauts in the original Mercury space programme. First-borns also make up a generous proportion of university professors, business executives, and Rhodes scholars. But while you are one of the do-it people of the world, you are likely to pay a price for it. Leman says that not only do first-borns and only children tend to get migraines, cluster headaches, and colitis, but they also form the bulk of the patients at his psychiatric clinic. Indeed, sex therapist Dagmar O'Connor says, 'The typical patient, and the typical first

child, is a high achiever. They always tried to please by working hard and getting the exam results that their parents
wanted. Part of that desire to please involves not allowing
themselves to have a sexual nature, bottling up their feelings because their parents may not like them.' She has found
that first-born women are often unable to reach orgasm and
that first-born men typically suffer from impotence.

If you are the second child but of the opposite sex, then
you are more likely to develop many of the first-born's personality characteristics than if you are of the same sex as
your elder sibling. And in the same way, you are more likely
to be a high achiever.

Middle children typically have the toughest time at home
because they get the least attention and not so much is
expected of them, which often makes them fractious and
gives them a feeling of alienation. They are also difficult to
categorize. 'About the only thing you can say is that a middle child will be influenced by whatever the child directly
above is like,' notes Leman. 'Whatever that may be, he will
typically shoot off in the opposite direction.' But while you
probably won't be a high achiever if you're a middle child,
you will avoid the high stress levels of the first-born and,
as a result, many of the physical ailments to which he or
she is prone. And because you were subject to less parental
pressure to conform and do well, while at the same time
experiencing more hard knocks, you will have benefited by
developing greater emotional stability than either the first-
born or the youngest child.

If you are the baby of the family you will have been cos-
seted and fussed over by your parents, yet at the same time
made very aware that you are the smallest and seemingly
the least important member of the family. In fact your older
brothers and sisters may have treated you like a baby, and
you will have had difficulty in gaining their attention. This
is why you may have developed into something of a clown,
in order to make them notice you by your jokes and risible
antics, or you may have learned to manipulate them and
others by being charming and persuasive. Indeed, this per-

haps explains why so many youngest children become comics, entertainers, estate agents, salesmen, ad-men, market traders, con-men, etc., who basically live by their wits. Hence it is not surprising that family babies tend to lack confidence, make themselves noticeable by adopting eccentric mannerisms and habits, or colourful dress styles, and are less honest, reliable and conventional than their older siblings.

Thinking back, did you grow up in a family whose members frequently expressed their affection for one another by touching? Or was touching taboo in your home? Touching is a form of communication, not simply because it helps to convey what we are feeling at the time, but because the way we touch often reveals the sort of people we are. So make a note of how you touch others and when you touch them, and then read on.

67

If you are the sort of person that rarely or never touches anyone else, then you almost certainly grew up in a family where there was little physical expression of affection, so that you never learned to touch. Hence you feel uncomfortable touching other people, even those to whom you are close, and you may not like being touched yourself. This does not mean that you lack affection or emotional warmth, as you probably compensate for your inability to touch by expressing how you feel in other ways, by giving presents, for example, or by giving strong verbal praise or encouragement, or if you are a boss, by rewarding your employees or those under you with pay rises, bonuses, and promotion.

But if, by contrast, you are a toucher, you may recognize your style of touching among the six described below, whose meaning is also considered.

1   **The gentle tapper**: here the touching takes the form

of light and tentative taps, which suggest a hesitancy in daring to touch at all. If your touching is like this it identifies you as a sensitive, yet shy person, who feels awkward about intruding upon another's personal space. You are probably kind, considerate and caring, yet your shyness means that you find communicating with others difficult.

2   **The backslapper**: as the name suggests, this touching takes the form often of enthusiastic backslapping, which seems to suggest friendliness and camaraderie. Yet backslapping is theatrical overkill, and should you be a backslapper you are really quite shy. Hence you have trouble in successfully interacting with others. And while your backslapping seems spontaneous, it is likely to be carefully rehearsed. Indeed, you have difficulty in taking life as it comes and enjoying each and every moment, but need to organize everything so that you know what's going to happen next. You fear the unexpected.

3   **The fingerprodder**: this form of touching involves pushing an extended finger, with varying degrees of force, into the arm or chest of another person, in order to make or emphasize a point. If this is your way of touching, it identifies you as a forceful and singleminded person, who is more interested in getting your views across than in considering the effect you might be having on the person you prod. You do not, in other words, have much social tact. However, your natural aggression and determination give you the ability to overcome difficulties and to achieve your goals.

4   **The massager**: here the touching takes the form of actual gripping and kneading of the arms, shoulders, etc., although in a non-sexual way. If you are a massager, you are likely to be a warm, uninhibited, affectionate, and sensual person. In fact you enjoy touching others, which enables you to express your interest in, and your concern for, them. But you are

not over-assertive and do not try to force your attentions on other people. In this respect you are guided by your innate sensitivity and intuition.

5 **The heavy rubber**: this type of touching involves rubbing instead of gripping or prodding, the hand being applied quite freely to the arms, shoulders and back. If you are a heavy rubber you are neither afraid of touching nor embarrassed by it. It shows you to be outgoing, open-hearted, honest and warm, with a liking for directness in your relationships. Because you are naturally enthusiastic and willing to take risks, you may go far in life or come badly unstuck. However, the person who is a heavy rubber must not be confused with the last type, whose touching has a quite different purpose.

6 **The domineering heavy rubber**: here the rubbing is used only as a method of putting a point of view or asserting an argument. If you use this touching technique, it reveals that you are unsure of yourself and your ideas, but that you hope to carry the day by adding physical pressure to what you say. Your touching is thus used as a means of dominating others, and is neither pleasant nor welcomed.

Lastly, you may have noticed that the personality of some short men is different from that of men of average height or above. Little men are often overly sensitive to slights, irascible, uppity and demanding, and are motivated by a desire to attain a position of power. This aggressive stance is known as the Napoleon complex and is caused, according to psychologist John Gillis, the author of *Too Short, Too Tall* (Institute of Personality and Ability, 1982), by their replacing 'feelings of inferiority with a drive for superiority'. Yet some short people manage to gain the attention that they need by developing verbal and social skills—by being funny or clever, or entertaining, for example—which is a much more positive way of coping with shortness than by becoming a bully. Self-esteem is also sought by being in the public eye, and because height can be gained by standing upon a stage, this explains why many actors and performers are small people. In fact studies of the undersized have shown that it is men below the height of 5'5" who are most likely to feel inferior. The average height of men in both Great Britain and the United States is 5'8".

The following is a list of famous short men: short men, that is, who have made it big.

Alexander the Great, world conqueror:	5'6"
Augustus Caesar, Roman emperor:	5'6"
Benjamin Harrison, U.S. president:	5'6"
Sylvester Stallone, U.S. film actor:	5'6"
The Duke of Windsor, formerly Edward VIII:	5'6"
Emile Zola, French author:	5'6"
T.E. Lawrence ('Lawrence of Arabia'), British soldier/author:	5'5½"
Adolf Hitler, German dictator:	5'5"
Alan Ladd, U.S. film star:	5'5"
H.G. Wells, British author:	5'5"
Sammy Davis, Jr., U.S. crooner:	5'4"
Michael J. Fox, U.S. film star:	5'4"
David Garrick, British actor-manager:	5'4"
James Madison, U.S. president:	5'4"
Benito Mussolini, Italian dictator:	5'4"
Honoré de Balzac, French author:	5'3"
Milton Friedman, U.S. economist:	5'3"
Elton John, British pop singer:	5'3"
Dudley Moore, British comedian:	5'2½"
Napoleon Bonaparte, French Emperor:	5'2"
Dustin Hoffman, U.S. film actor:	5'2"
Wayne Sleep, British dancer:	5'2"
James Boswell, British biographer:	5'1"
Danny DeVito, U.S. film actor:	5'1"
Edward Grieg, Norwegian Composer:	5'1"
Henri de Toulouse-Lautrec, French painter:	5'1"
Deng Xiao Ping, Chinese leader:	4'11"
William Shoemaker, U.S. Jockey:	4'11"
Alexander Pope, British poet:	4'6"

Arrian records that following Alexander the Great's defeat of the Persian king Darius at the battle of Issus, the Macedonian conqueror visited the tent occupied by Darius's captured mother, wife and children, accompanied only by his favourite Hephaestion, 'and that Darius's mother, in doubt, owing to the similarity of their dress, which of the two was the King, prostrated herself before Hephaestion, because he was taller than his companion but Alexander merely remarked that her error was of no account, for Hephaestion, too, was an Alexander—a 'protector of men'. The conqueror of Asia clearly had no hang-ups about his lack of height.

Chapter Ten

DRAWING TESTS

Search then the RULING PASSION: there, alone
The Wild are constant, and the Cunning known;
The Fool consistent, and the False sincere;
Priests, Princes, Women, no dissemblers here.

In an earlier chapter it was noted how the drawing of doodles can reveal aspects of the personality that may normally be kept hidden. In this chapter the use of drawings is taken a step further, by giving you three tests to complete that involve them. Each will give information about different aspects of your personality. In fact we shall use drawings to determine your telephone personality; your attitude to the past, the present, and the future; and your feelings about your home background, your parents, your path through life, sex, etc.

Early in 1989 Dr David Lewis wrote a booklet for British Telecom, in which he advised subscribers how to make best use of the telephone. Most people, he said, belong to one of four personality groups where their telephone technique is concerned, and by identifying what it is early in the call you can use the knowledge to your advantage. But what about yourself? Which group do you belong to? This can be easily discovered by choosing the symbol which most appeals to you from the four shown in Figure 29.

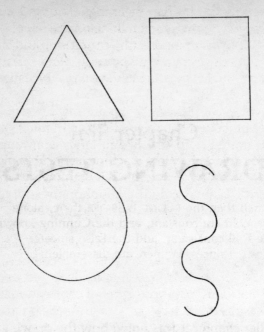

Figure 29: Symbols indicative of your personality type

_____ **68** _____

If you selected the triangle it identifies you as an Aspirer. You have goals to reach, so you're in something of a hurry. Quite probably you knew what you wanted to achieve early in life and have concentrated on fulfilling your ambitions ever since. When using the telephone you tend to be brisk and to the point, and you may cut off the other person without further ado once you've said your piece: you certainly won't want to engage in aimless social chat. You not only speak quickly but probably have the impatient habit of completing other people's sentences for them.

If, however, you chose the circle, it reveals you to be the warm and sociable Admirer type. You are blessed with considerable skill in handling people, especially as you can often sense things that aren't obvious, or read between words, so to speak, to discern hidden meanings. You find it hard to keep solely to the point when talking on the telephone, but like to enquire about the health, condition, and mood of the person to whom you are speaking. And because you sound happy and seem interested, you're a pleasure to talk to.

Should you have picked the square in preference to the other three symbols, it shows you to be an Inquirer. You have an objective mind, and you like to analyse any problems carefully and at length before reaching a conclusion or making a decision. You are therefore a slow, sure type, who hates to be hurried. When using the telephone you are not interested in social chatter, and your style of speaking is calm and thoughtful. You may dry up when you're thinking, which can result in some uncomfortable silences from the other person's point of view. You seldom become emotional about anything, as you believe that leads to bad decisions.

Lastly, if the squiggle is your symbol choice, it marks you out as an Inspirer. You have a lot of enthusiasm and sparkle, and you love new ideas and fresh challenges, as these create the variety that stops your life from becoming dull and boring. Indeed, you are blessed with plenty of energy, which you tend to show in the rushed, excited, and almost breathless manner in which you speak. You can cope with more than one idea at the same time, enjoy going out and having a good time, and you probably have many friends.

The next drawing test requires you to do just that, so you'll need a blank sheet of paper and a pen or pencil. The test was devised by Professor Frederick Koenig at Tulane University in the United States, and it will reveal your subconscious attitudes to life. All you have to do is draw three circles, of any size and positioned how you like, on the paper, one to represent the past, one the present, and one the future. Mark them in some way so that you know which is meant to be which. Do this before reading on.

A person's attitude to life, says Professor Koenig, is usually orientated towards either the past, the present, or the future, and he adds, 'We know that things that are drawn larger by people are seen by them as being more important.' Hence when one of the circles is drawn larger than the others, it reveals that the time period it signifies—past, present or future—is considered to be of prime importance. In this respect it identifies you as being backward-looking, or preoccupied with the present, or forward-looking. And clearly, if the largest circle is much bigger than the other two, it shows that a special emphasis is placed on the time period in question, whereas if the size difference is not that great, then the emphasis placed upon that period of time is not that great either.

The spacing or position of the circles one to another must next be examined. Are they completely separate? Or do they touch or perhaps overlap? If you have drawn your three circles quite separate from each other, it reveals that you see the past, the present, and the future as themselves being separate from one another, each having little influence on the other. However, if you have drawn touching or overlapping circles, then you see the past, the present and the future as a continuum. 'The person who views his life as such a continuous process,' comments Professor Koenig, 'is a person who, as a rule, has control over his destiny'.

69

1 If you have drawn three circles of approximately the same size that are not touching, they identify you as a reasonably stable person with an easy-going attitude to life. 'You're flexible rather than rigid,' says Professor Koenig. 'You don't have any big, important goals for the future and you don't feel guilty, or suffer regrets, about what happened in the past. You by and large take each day as it comes, accept other people at their face value, and seldom hold grudges.'

2 But if the circle representing the past is the largest of the three, it indicates that your family and your

background are particularly important to you. You may even feel that your best years have come and gone. Temperamentally, you're a thoughtful person who values your privacy and who has learned lessons from your past mistakes.

3 If the circle representing the present is the biggest, it shows that you are fully occupied with today, to the extent that you probably wish you had more time to do all that you want. Because you make the most of your present opportunities, you have little or no interest in mulling over past events or yearning for what might happen one day.

4 Should the circle representing the future be drawn larger than the other two, it reveals that you are an optimist who thinks that life will improve for you as time goes by. This is why you're prepared to forgo pleasure now in order to achieve greater satisfaction in the future. You certainly do not believe that 'tomorrow never comes'.

5 If the smallest circle you have drawn is the one representing the past, it signifies that you are probably a self-made man or woman. You are satisfied with what you have thus far achieved and have confidence in your future prospects. Indeed, if you are a woman, then you're probably happily married.

6 But if the circle representing the present is the smallest of the three, it shows that you are an intellectual, with logical thought processes, who lets his head rule his heart. Professor Koenig says that you're also inquisitive, a lover of culture, and probably a heavy reader.

7 If you have drawn the three circles standing on top of one another in a column, then you are the rare person who feels that time has come to a stop. This may be because you have recently suffered a personal tragedy.

Professor Koenig has found that the largest proportion of

those who have taken his test are present-orientated, and
that very few people are backward-looking. About 50 per
cent of college students, he has noticed, draw overlapping
circles, which means that they regard time as continuous.

For the next, and last, drawing test take a plain sheet of paper
and on it draw a scene made up of the following images:
a house, a tree, a path, a pond, a snake, a bush, and the
sun. These should be arranged how you like and each drawn
to the size that you feel is best. It is your drawing, so please
yourself.

When you have completed the drawing, you can read on.

70

This test is designed to help you discover more about your
basic attitudes and feelings, and thus provides an overview
of your personality. This explains why you have been asked
to draw the images in question, for they are all archetypes
symbolizing essential aspects of yourself. The house signifies your home, the pond your mother, the sun your father,
the bush your friends, the tree your ambition, the path your
life, and the snake your sexual urges.

The first thing to do is to note the size of each of the
images, then their positions relative to one another, and lastly
the degree of attention that they each receive. As we have
previously discovered, an object that is drawn large in size
and with perhaps greater attention to detail than are the
others, for example, testifies to the importance of the person, attitudes or feelings that it symbolizes, and vice versa.
The interpretation of the drawing shown in Figure 30 will
help you to analyse your own.

All the images in the drawing are boldly and clearly drawn,
which immediately suggests a lack of embarrassment or disquiet about the attitudes symbolized, although the pond,
representing the mother, is only shown in part, revealing
that her influence in the person's life, while important, has
been 'pushed to one side' or is considered to be less

Figure 30: Scene drawn by volunteer subject

important than it actually is. The sun, on the other hand, is placed quite high in the sky and shown shining brightly, indicating that the father is well-regarded and perhaps given more credit than is his due, its actual size being much smaller than the pond. The sun also gives an insight into the person's view of himself, and shows that this is positive and vibrant.

The house is quite large and is centrally placed, yet only has one floor, indicating that the home environment, while solid in the sense of offering firm and sensible beliefs, did not provide much opportunity of expanding the subject's horizons. Yet despite this, or perhaps because of it, the home gave the subject a strong desire to advance himself. Smoke rises from the chimney, suggesting that an ascent could be imagined by the subject, while a plant, symbolic of creativity, climbs the front wall. Likewise, the path leads from the house, revealing that a way forward in life was provided by the home situation. The path, evidently one made of gravel, is shown as a thing of substance, thereby reflecting a positive attitude to life, and makes its way directly towards the observer, widening markedly as it passes the pond, and so showing that life has become fuller and more enriching for the subject in recent years. And interestingly enough, the path's outline reflects that of the tree; indeed, the path could almost be a shadow of the tree, suggesting that the subject's views about life go hand-in-glove with the fulfilment of his ambitions. Thus as he becomes more successful, so his feelings about life become more buoyant.

The tree is the largest and most dominant image in the drawing, although it is in balance with the size of the house, and reveals that the subject's ambitions—his desire to get ahead and make something of himself—are considerable. The tree's trunk is shown upright and straight, betokening a lack of deviousness and dishonesty in his nature, and hence a desire to get ahead in an honourable way. The many branches growing from the tree trunk symbolize several talents and indicate that he is not limited to one ability in order to fulfil himself. However, the tree's foliage is only sketchily drawn, which means that he has not yet fulfilled himself creatively. The bush placed close to the tree indicates that his friendships have largely been made through his work, yet its small size and the fact that it is placed at the side of the picture suggest that they are not all that important to him, although the bush's foliage reveals a friendly personality.

The snake is portrayed uncoiled and out in the open, and is placed in the foreground. It is also of modest size. Indeed, it is a rather friendly-looking snake. It shows that the subject's sexual desires, while of more immediate importance than, say, his friendships or even his ambitions, are uncomplicated and of a moderate dimension. He has no guilt about them. In fact where his sexual attitudes and desires are concerned he has nothing to hide.

If you now consider your drawing in a similar way, you will just as easily be able to uncover your attitudes and preoccupations, which will in turn give you a better understanding of yourself.

AFTERWORD

If you have read through this book from the beginning and have taken note of what is said, and have done what is asked of you, you will have few, if any, personal secrets left to discover. Hence you will, to a large extent, know yourself.

The methods you have used to gain such self-knowledge can be employed with equal success on others, which will enable you to understand them, and perhaps to get on with them, better. In this way a little more happiness may be introduced into the world.

In his *Memorabilia*, Xenophon records a conversation which took place between Socrates and a young man named Euthydemus, on the subject of self-knowledge. I shall leave you with what Socrates, whom the Delphic oracle proclaimed as the wisest and the most just man in all Greece, said about the practical benefits of being so enlightened.

Socrates asked him if he had ever been at Delphi, and Euthydemus answered that he had been there twice.

'Did you take notice,' said Socrates, 'that somewhere on the front of the temple there is this inscription, KNOW THYSELF?'

He answered, 'I remember I have read it there.'

'It is not enough,' replied Socrates, 'to have read it. Have you been the better for this admonition? Have you given yourself the trouble to consider what you are?'

'I think I know that well enough,' replied the young man, 'for I should have found it very difficult to have known any other thing, if I had not known myself.'

'But for a man to know himself well,' said Socrates, 'it is not enough that he knows his own name: for as a man that buys a horse cannot be certain that he knows what he is, before he has ridden him, to see whether he be quiet or restive, whether he be mettlesome or dull, whether he be fleet or heavy; in short, before he has made a trial of all that is good and bad in him, in like manner a man cannot say that he knows himself, before he has tried what he is fit for, and what he is able to do.'

'It is true,' said Euthydemus, 'that whoever knows not his own strength, knows not himself.'

'But,' continued Socrates, 'who sees not of how great advantage this knowledge is to man, and how dangerous it is to be mistaken in this affair: for he who knows himself, knows likewise what is good for himself. He sees what he is able to do, and what he is not able to do. By applying himself to things that he can do, he gets his bread with pleasure, and is happy: and by not attempting to do the things he cannot do, he avoids the danger of falling into errors, and of seeing himself miserable. By knowing himself, he knows likewise how to judge of others, and to make use of their services for his own advantage, either to procure himself some good, or to protect himself from some misfortune. But he who knows not himself, and is mistaken in the opinion he has of his own abilities, mistakes likewise in the knowledge of others, and in the conduct of his own affairs. He is ignorant of what is necessary for him, he knows not what he undertakes, nor comprehends the means he makes use of, and this is the reason that success never attends his enterprises, and that he always falls into misfortunes. But the man who sees clear into his own designs, generally obtains the end he proposes to himself, and at the same time gains reputation and honour. For this reason even his equals are well pleased to follows his advice; and they whose affairs are in disorder, implore his assistance, and throw themselves into his hands, depending upon his prudence to retrieve their former welfare.'

INDEX